healed enough

"The author has portrayed her journey of trauma and recovery in such a way that I found myself tapping into the parts of me that were ready to 'come home' and find settling. This book is a beautiful experience."

MICHAEL YASINKSI, MD

"Chelsey's story brings to life some of the darkest places the human body and spirit can reside. A place where abuse and neglect, including that from ourselves, can bring us to believe we were meant for that chaos. Most importantly, she shares how that veil of darkness can be lifted, how that formerly bent body and spirit can *thrive* in a world filled with light.

This is a story of truth, of grit and determination, and of authentic hope. It is perfect for trauma survivors and the clinicians, family, and friends who truly support them."

ANNE K., Exec. Director, Beauty After Bruises

"This memoir is a beautifully brave unveiling of a life shaped by hidden wounds and the long journey back to oneself. Chelsey writes with a vulnerability that is both raw and deeply compassionate, illuminating the subtle ways trauma shapes identity, relationships, and self-perception."

CASSANDRA VAN VOORHEES, LPC

healed enough

A MEMOIR

A Journey through Complex
Trauma and Dissociation

CHELSEY VALERI, LCSW

Published by

MANDALA
TREE PRESS
mandalatreepress.com

ISBN 978-1-968242-05-3 (paperback KDP)
ISBN 978-1-968242-06-0 (case laminate KDP)
ISBN 978-1-968242-07-7 (paperback LSI)
ISBN 978-1-968242-08-4 (case laminate LSI)
ISBN 978-1-968242-04-6 (ebook)

SEL043000   SELF-HELP / Post-Traumatic Stress Disorder (PTSD)
PSY075000   PSYCHOLOGY / Trauma Psychology
BIO026000   BIOGRAPHY & AUTOBIOGRAPHY / Memoirs

Edited and designed by Kaitlin Barwick

www.chelseyvaleri.com

To the woman I am today. The one who experienced
the trauma, carried the pain, and learned to
survive through different versions of me.

To my beautiful boys. Your hearts remind me
every day that this healing is possible.

And to my husband—thank you for loving all of me.

contents

prologue

We had just moved into our new house—me, my husband, our infant son, and two dogs. The Arizona sunshine lit up our master room. Kyle sat at his work desk against the window overlooking the green grass and inground pool of our spacious yard when I approached him and sat on his lap without hesitation. He welcomed my presence wordlessly, comfortingly, as he always did.

It started with an uncomfortable warmth, a slow spreading burn in my chest followed by a crawling sensation through my stomach. Without warning, my body shrank, my limbs felt small, and I was no longer a grown woman sitting on my husband's lap.

I was a little girl again, and the man under me was dangerous.

An overwhelming wave of terror crashed through me. But in a matter of seconds—that felt like eons—the fear vanished, and I was shifted back into a body that felt more familiar. As I slowly blinked my eyes, I could see our room, the grass through the large bay window, and the man in front of me as my husband, innocently oblivious to my brief panic as he tapped away at his keyboard.

I had no emotional connection to what was happening; it felt like I was viewing my life through a third-party lens, peering in on someone else's intimate moment. I tried to remind myself that I was sitting on *Kyle's* lap: the man I chose to marry, who had always been safe. So why did I feel such imminent danger?

My therapist brain kicked in and I knew what it was: a dissociative experience. But still, *why?* I started to intellectualize the possibilities behind such symptoms but was quickly halted by denial. My thoughts raced. *I don't have memory of this type of event. Who would it even be who abused me in early childhood?* Unable to recall a specific event, I ended with, *It must be related to later in life sexual abuse.*

The level of nonrealization flipped on like a light switch and protected me in all the ways it had before. After a moment, the anxiety dissipated and I continued with my day, emotionally removed from the intense somatic event I had just endured. Masking in this type of way came as easily to me as drinking water. My ability to "switch states" was quite remarkable, shocking to others at the time but completely second nature to me. I could continue parenting, taking care of our dogs, and setting up our new house without a pause, even as my mind was in turmoil.

I'd taken up hot yoga at a studio in a hip new area of Denver three years earlier. Practicing yoga was the closest I would get to mindfulness at that time in my life without becoming engulfed with panic. Looking for that calm I hadn't truly felt for days, I was lying down at the end of class, one hand on my stomach and the other on my chest, feeling my breath slowing down and deepening the connection I had to my own body—then bam.

The flashes came quickly, one after another: a snapshot of feeling scared, frozen, with adult hands where they did not belong and a brief image of a man's face, spinning through my mind in a whirlwind of fear, never lingering long enough to absorb concrete detail. At first, I wished the memory would go away, but then I became obsessed about what it meant. My body in the present moment started shaking, letting me know that the memory must have some validity. My brain spun like a rolodex, taunting me with fleeting images of being in a classroom alone with this man, then another of me standing paralyzed by fear beside him with other adults in the room. I started to recall the handful of times I had seen him around our small city at various points throughout my childhood, each memory accompanied by a hollowness in my chest.

I left the yoga studio shaking. *What do I do now?*

On my drive home, I called my therapist who I had been seeing for a few months. Thankfully, she answered my call, and I parked on the side of the gravel road that lead to our house. While I don't remember exactly what she said to me, she did validate the symptoms I was experiencing in conjunction with memories related to sexual abuse. She didn't bombard me with questions or seek out unnecessary details. She held space for what my body needed, and that was to rid myself of the yuckiness that had taken over my entire body. My skin crawled. I wanted to peel it off and grow a new layer, something that didn't trap the feelings of being violated.

After we hung up, I drove another block up the street and pulled into our driveway. I called my husband and asked him to come out and help me get from my car into our house. This ritual was not new to us; ever since I had gotten sober, I could not get out of the car alone and walk to my doorstep, especially in the dark—it wasn't because I was hindered physically but because I was stuck in psychological torture.

As soon as we crossed through the front door of our condo, I walked straight down the hallway, ignoring our cat's meow, and fled directly to our room. I crawled into bed, bringing the sheets and comforter up past my chin and blankly staring at the nightside table. It felt too dangerous to avert my eyes elsewhere and attempt to connect with anyone, even Kyle. I stared there in a dissociative state for hours.

It took me many additional months to acknowledge what these experiences probably meant; my body was remembering something I cognitively couldn't. This very notion was too much to accept, so I hid behind a different version of myself and bottled up my personal trauma.

I buried myself in motherhood, treating my clients who had similar histories and experiences, attending clinical trainings, and anything else that felt less dangerous than recognizing aspects of my own trauma. I rationalized that being sober provided me with safer people, a less chaotic day-to-day life, and a life truly beyond my wildest dreams—so I convinced myself that digging into the past too much was not beneficial. It would hit me like a freight train at times: staying sober had not healed the past wounds that greatly influenced my substance abuse and self-destructive behaviors in the first place.

I reached a point in my life where it was necessary to gain a foundational understanding of why my mind and body felt so haunted. Without moving forward in some way, I feared that I was going to be stuck in the continuous cycle of emotional distress, flashbacks, hypervigilance, and rage forever.

What I *did* know was that it was hard to be stuck in my body. The profound exhaustion told me so. Many days, I would ask myself why I was so tired, without any recognition of the reasons why. Between the somatic indications related to sexual abuse, the imbalance of my blood sugars due to type 1 diabetes, my chronically dysregulated nervous system, and the internal management of everything, I was depleted. However, I had developed a significant ability to "continue on" regardless of these realities.

PART ONE

growing up

THE UNKNOWN

While I have very few memories, positive or negative, throughout a lot of my developmental years, I do know that I often felt trapped within myself and deeply self-conscious about who I was. In early childhood years, I was described as a confident, bossy, and independent child, but as I entered adolescence, those qualities faded away and were replaced by uncertainty, mistrust, and emotional distress. I constantly twisted my hair, looked over my shoulder, judged every statement that came out of my mouth, and was hypervigilant to those around me.

I was always mystified when I saw other girls my age appearing confident, comfortable, and effortlessly in charge of their movements. I desperately wanted to feel the freedom that they displayed, but it felt intolerable. Even laughing freely became something I was self-conscious of. When I walked into a room, my face was often blank yet protective, my body humming with an underlying vibration that felt unsafe and a mind that felt crowded with various parts of myself. This state was certainly one that led to me wanting to crawl into a different body, and since I couldn't do that, I locked away parts of me that no one could access. It felt like the safer option.

To be transparent, most people around me would never have guessed I felt this way. I was part of the "popular" and "mean girl" crowd in both middle and high school, something that plagues me with guilt today. I now see how much direct and indirect harm I caused to others because of my own wounding and disruptive, bulldozing behavior.

In middle school, I discovered that alcohol helped the pervasive sense of emptiness that was becoming me. It boosted my ability to "let go" and appear "free, daring, and fun"—all attributes that I did not feel were a part of my makeup. When I felt the warm liquid going down my throat and the rush of it through my body, I was able to let out a notable exhale. Deep down, this experience filled me with anxiety because I knew my reaction to alcohol at twelve years old was not typical.

Throughout this book, I discuss several early life experiences that influenced the way I felt in my family, in my community, and internally. While I cannot pinpoint one incident that dimmed my internal joy and sense of freedom, I assume that the accumulation of events did. While I may appear confident in expressing the impact that events and complex dynamics had on who I developed into, I spent many years in complete darkness and disconnection from the reality that I had experienced *anything*.

Regrettably, I even judged those who spoke out about childhood and traumatic life events because of how uncomfortable I felt in the face of their vulnerability. I never experienced people holding adequate space for difficult conversations or mature topics; I often watched my own parents squirm at any sort of difficult dialogue. It was easier for me to connect to a song, a TV show, or a movie—something I had no responsibility to respond to but that made my tears flow easier.

As I grew older, I found myself dismissing stories that others told, partially because I was so disconnected from the events that happened to me and emotions that stemmed from them. I consistently downplayed the impact of childhood experiences on my development because of common thought patterns such as, *It could have been worse, At least this didn't happen to me*, or *It's over now, time to move on*. Most of my memories would appear like a flash in my mind or like scenes in a movie, hardly "proof" of anything.

Over the years, I spent a significant amount of time flipping through my yellow, cloud-covered childhood photo album, tracing my mom's handwriting next to each photo, meticulously documenting the year and location of each picture. Seeing this dedication always gave me a warm sensation in my stomach. She really was attentive in many ways to us kids.

But the album also highlighted the yawning chasm between who I was in youth and who I had grown into as a young adult. In many of the early pictures, I could see myself smiling and seemingly enjoying whatever I was doing, but as I flipped more pages and moved forward in time, I watched as my big smile faded into a neutral face, one that mirrored my internal uncertainty. Despite the timeline of events that my parents maintained in multiple heartwarming albums, I felt wholly disconnected from the little girl in the pictures. She looked like me, had my blue eyes and dirty blonde hair, my slight shyness in her smile, and matching freckles sprinkled on her face, but my recognition of this version of me was blurry at best. I knew I had lived a life before things took a turn for the worst, out of control and dangerous, but it felt intolerable to connect to the younger version of myself.

Despite our appearance as a typical middle class suburbia family, the emotional consistency and safety we truly needed was either inconsistent or completely missing. The dynamics at home were dysfunctional; the fallout from my parents' unhealed generational trauma impacted their marriage, their parenting, and the way they treated themselves.

Things weren't awful at home, which I thought was the only prerequisite to have a good enough "reason" to be impacted negatively by your childhood. I am lucky enough to say that I had two parents who loved my brother and me very much, but at times, they parented through a faulty lens.

I grew up in Southern Alberta, Canada, in between the Rocky Mountains and the prairies. We had many close family friends. In my early years, we spent hours together with other families, including holidays, birthdays, and weekends. My brother and I had the perfect matching outfits and the idyllic themed family pictures. All our needs were met and some of our wants. What was consistently missing from my memory were stable emotional connections among all of us.

My parents struggled immensely to show love to one another. Witnessing them try and fail to navigate their connection gave me constant unease. I don't think I really knew what I was seeing at the time, but as I grew, my understanding deepened, and I could easily sense when things were heightened at home; the tension would hang around the air like thick smog, impossible to breathe through. My brother and I would glance at one another, give a nod, and retreat to a different room, one that was calmer.

Both my mom and dad had unresolved childhood wounds and personal struggles that impacted their parenting approaches. In adulthood, many stories have been shared with me about the dynamics in their marriage and their personal struggles, including alcohol abuse, infidelity, rage, and codependency—all of which my body has held onto the felt sense of.

A HOUSE ON EGGSHELLS

My dad's new job moved our family out of Calgary, Alberta, to Saskatoon, Saskatchewan. He worked out of the home in my early years and often had to travel, leaving my mom at home, in a new city—with me and pregnant with my younger brother—with no family or friend support. My mom provided a predictable but rigid home environment In those first several years of our childhood. There was very little room for error. My brother and I appeared flawless and were expected to behave in a way that matched our appearance. While my mom was an involved and dedicated mother who loved her children deeply, the felt sense of rigidity and anxiety rubbed off on me as I grew.

After two short years in Saskatoon, we moved back to Alberta as a family of four, when I was about preschool age. From what I was told, my family seemingly thrived being back in Lethbridge, Alberta, with close friends and family nearby. My dad was a physically active and fun dad. We spent time outside, hiking, biking, and frolicking in our yard. However, emotional vulnerability and heartfelt discussions from him were not common. Over the years, I would be witness to many intense emotions from my him, mostly anger and rage. But between these outbursts, there would be playfulness and joy, especially when we were around others. As I grew into primary school years, I began to recognize that both of my parents presented starkly different to the external world than they did at home as a family.

The nervousness and confusion I often felt during my dad's displays of intensity was overwhelming to navigate as a young kid. The sharpness in his voice would cause an immediate gut reaction; my stomach would tighten, and my fingertips would tingle with dread. I learned to tiptoe around him. I could sense his mood and emotions well by the time I was a preteen. At some point, I came to fear my dad's responses not only to me but to others; there were many outbursts over the years, toward my brother, my mom, strangers, and other people close to us that left me feeling humiliated.

Contrary to the one side of my dad, he was also the parent we played sports with, the one we laughed with the most, and the one who would engage in roughhousing with my brother and me. I knew my dad loved us more than anyone else is the world, but his inability to regulate his emotional state led to a push-and-pull dynamic. I wanted my dad's attention and loved him deeply, but I was also always on edge, looking for signs of the next outburst. There was always a sense that the fun version of him would be fleeting because of the short fuse he lived with.

When I was eleven years old, my grandfather took his last breath while my dad held this hand. His death destroyed my dad emotionally. There were rows of chairs set up in my grandparents' house for the small funeral, and I sat in the back, watching my dad's shoulders move up and down as he sobbed. I felt frozen. I had never witnessed this type of emotion in my dad before and had no idea how to respond. It was like his sadness was being dumped into my backpack with an expectation for me to carry it, and that felt inconceivable.

At the same time of my grandfather's death, my parents' marriage was falling apart. There had been infidelity. My dad drank too much as a way of coping. My mom appeared emotionally void and angry. They eventually had to file for financial bankruptcy. While I was spared the details of these events as a kid, I felt the chaotic energy in our home and the unpredictability of what was going to happen next.

In their own way, I believe that my parents tried to make their marriage work, but with their limited insight and lack of support and resources, the world worked against them. There were several times when I encountered both of my parents in a state of complete despair over losing one another, but in the next moment, the would be avoidant and angry again. At that age, I did not possess the maturity or experience to understand the complexities of marriage, and it was certainly not discussed in depth because of the uncomfortableness such topics seemingly caused in everyone.

UNANCHORED

Despite our parents' shared love for my brother and me, their divorce was inevitable. The whispers about my dad's affair started trickling down from the parents of my friends and acquaintances in school until they reached my ears. I was in middle school at the time, and my friend group rapidly grew to include other girls and boys from other schools. I sensed the whispering and gossip about my family from other kids, tying my stomach into knots. I was baffled at how others seemed to know about my family's darkest secrets when my parents still hadn't confirmed a thing to their own children. It came easy to me, pretending that everything was okay—because that's what I watched both of my parents do every single day.

I was twelve years old when it was finalized. As a teen and in my early twenties, I was insistent that the divorce was not distressing to me, let alone traumatic; I even went as far as to say it was for the best and that we were happier as a family after the divorce. I think this was what I felt obligated to report, to appear strong and stable to those around me and to avoid my parents feeling bad about what they did. Simultaneously, if I were to listen to a song that was centered around marital discord or family chaos, I would be in a puddle of tears. I could never let anyone see me this way, quickly wiping away my tears and putting on a mask of neutrality.

We were dragged through consistent moving. While I don't remember places we lived or the process of packing of up our belongings in each one, I do recall the emotional impact would occasionally hit me like a gut punch. The loneliness often crept in during the evening hours when a part of my deeply desired family connection, a sit-down meal at the table, and a "family movie night" (something I don't remember ever experiencing). While we never yearned for more food or materialistic things, the emotional foundation of a home was missing. Yet, at the time, no adult in my life made a fuss about what my family was going through, so neither did I.

Honestly, the word "home" is difficult for me to connect to. I remember two homes from my childhood that felt "homey"; the other thirteen-plus were completely forgettable. After the divorce, there was no sense of stability regarding a "home" between either of my parents; the moves were endless. My brother and I have counted as adults, and by the time we were teenagers, we lived in approximately fifteen different townhomes, duplexes, or homes.

I have always joked that moving a lot in childhood made my wild teenage years more tolerable. I learned to sleep anywhere, including random apartments and dirty party houses, and I could easily feel at "home" in any of my friends' family homes. Despite my seeming flexibility, I did experience moments of homesickness, yearning for the welcoming smell of where my mom lived, the absurdly comfy old black leather couch that followed my dad, or the knowledge that I could go to sleep at night without anything happening to me. I spent many nights away from home terrified of the environment I was in, the possibilities of what could happen, but whenever I thought of asking either of my parents to come get me, the words would stick in my throat.

As we got older and my mom's adult life grew more complicated, her rigidity turned into avoidance and emotional absence. Despite always having a safe place to go, a warm bed to sleep in, and food in the fridge, I deeply felt the lonely distance of that missing element of togetherness. As a teenager, I never really knew when I was going to see my mom. Of course, we still had our mom-and-daughter shopping dates and other surface ways we knew how to connect with one another, but it felt like we were living hundreds of miles apart on an emotional level. Deep down, I really missed her. No matter how much I pushed her away and told her I hated her, I desperately needed the comfort of her homemade cookies, her chicken soup when I was sick, and our once weekly ritual of watching *So You Think You Can Dance?* or *Intervention*.

After her divorce from my dad, my mom started dating and spent majority of her time split between work and the new man in her life. Eventually, she met my now-stepdad and spent much of her time at his home, leaving my brother and I home alone. She felt like a different person when she was with her new partner. From my view, she met his every request and emotional need, putting herself and her kids on the back burner.

Spending time with the two of them felt like I was walking on eggshells. I didn't know how to be myself around him and this new dynamic. I was often reminded by my mom and him that since she worked full time, she deserved a break and time to relax instead of "worrying about us kids." I remember being told that we were old enough to "take care of ourselves." This approach completely disregarded any emotional need my brother and I had, and it eroded any safety I felt with my mom.

Every statement like those was a punch to my gut, driving my feelings of guilt deeper with every repetition. Why did she need (or want) a break from her kids when she rarely saw us due to work? I couldn't understand why the meticulous, put-together woman I'd known as my mom was now seemingly struggling immensely in her role as our caretaker while simultaneously caving in to anything her new partner needed or wanted instead. Pretty quickly, it felt like we were all strangers sharing space for a few days a week. Most days, she came and went from the house in minutes. I rarely remember having dinner with my mom at any point in my teens. Anything I could reheat or microwave became my go-to dinner option until I forced myself to learn how to use a stove.

My brother and I went back and forth to my dad's every week or two, but we were met with similar dynamics there: a parent who worked hard and was away from home a lot and a new stepparent who I rejected almost immediately. My brother retreated to his room to play video games and smoke weed while I frantically searched for connection with my friends, boys, and substances.

Some nights, I was able to find solace in my dad's basement, where the comfortable, lived-in black leather couch sat, coupled with familiar blankets from my childhood. My dad was a pro at not throwing items away and kept meaningful things that represented various periods of our life. Many of these items moved with us all those times throughout years, attempting to represent a home life that was not together at all.

As I got older, my brother and I struggled with significant rage. There were doors and walls punched, consistent screaming, things thrown, and an overarching need to protect ourselves from one another. I distinctly remember many times when I would be cruel with my words only to have him physically come after me as I sprinted up the stairs to find a room where I could lock the door. He would violently pound on the door, shaking it, threatening to break it down.

Other days, I would be doing the same thing to him. These events heightened in frequency when we both lived with our mom as teenagers. She was almost always gone from the home, either working or dating. If she was around for aggressive episodes between my brother and me, she would scream at us before running upstairs to her room to lock the door.

Each time I heard her door slam, my stomach sank. Did she not know how to parent us in this state, or was it that she didn't want to at all? The truth probably fell somewhere in between. These moments of emotional separation from my mom led to more and more physical separateness and an increasing desire to run away.

A SENSE OF RELIEF

I was pacing in my bedroom, knowing there was a party going on that the older kids were throwing for the yearly celebration of Canada Day. I knew there would be alcohol, and I desperately wanted to go experience the escapism that I knew it could provide. I eventually mustered the courage to go ask my dad, who was sitting on the couch with his girlfriend, if I could go to the party with my best friends. There was no discussion about it: the answer was no. I felt defeated. How would I ever get my hands on something to help with my unbearable anxiety?

Over the years, I had observed what alcohol did for people. Through my young eyes, I saw the emotional freedom in provided my dad, my grandparents, and my parents' friends. We would attend parties with my parents often in childhood, and the rooms would be flooded with laughter, tipsy adults mingling without a care in the world. Occasionally there would be a marital spat, but alcohol seemed to drown out the intensity for the time being.

I did figure out how to take my first drink shortly after Canada Day. I don't remember the specific details of where and when it was, but I do know that I loved the effect of it. I could instantly feel the warmth of the alcohol filtering through my body, and I exhaled with a knowledge that I was going to be okay. I quickly learned that I felt better as drunk

Chelsey. I didn't care what others thought about me quite as much as I did sober, and (God forbid) if I experienced embarrassment or shame while intoxicated, the next drink usually drowned those emotions.

By the time I was fourteen years old, I desired a drink or drug almost every single day. Mind you, it was hard to find weed or alcohol at age fourteen, but my friends and I managed to get our hands on substances quite often. I explored self-harming with cutting for a short period, but I did it more so in hopes that someone would pay attention or notice how I felt rather than because I felt suicidal. Marijuana became a regular part of my life as well, hiding in alleys in the suburbs, sharing cigarettes and joints with other young teens who craved the escapism just as much as I did.

Soon came the days of sneaking out basement windows with my friends. After quietly jumping the backyard fence, we would run as fast as we could, elated at our newfound freedom. Next, we would find the perfect school field to drown our feelings away with whiskey or Canadian coolers. We would sometimes meet boys there or older siblings' friends, but often, it was just us girls, seeking connection and a longing to feel anything but the distress that seemed to consume us. To get home, we would often call a taxi from a nearby payphone and then have the driver drop us off three houses down from our own, running away without paying and jumping backyard fences until we reached our spot for the night.

As I reflect on these escapades, I realize that all of us were escaping unwanted feelings and chasing something that we were not getting at home. We were caught several times by one of our parents, but that didn't stop the behavior; if anything, it fueled it. While I remember being grounded and scolded for my actions, I don't recall the consequence having any impact on my decision to disengage in the behavior.

My desire to escape myself was too strong for my parents to control; I had officially turned into a wild child. Let me be clear—we had so many fun times. Despite our recklessness, nothing beat parties in random farmers' fields, the local skate park, and school playgrounds. Our secrets were mostly safe with us because there were no cell phones to document anything, and better yet, there was no social media. This era of my life predated the current age of instant digital memories. If we were lucky, someone would get a handful of worthy pictures on their disposable camera, one that took weeks to develop.

In between our drinking and partying, my friends and I found different hobbies including shoplifting and sneaking into abandoned homes. Eventually, people started to call the cops on us, and we were often chased away from public places where they found us drinking underage, vandalizing equipment, and leaving a mess of cigarettes and alcohol bottles. We laughed off these experiences as rites of passage into high school. Fortunately, there was a touch of innocence left in us at this point, and I had not yet crossed the bridge into the dark world of severe drug addiction.

HISTORY REPEATS

Both of my parents grew up in alcoholic homes. Because of this, not raising my brother and me in an alcoholic home was very important to them. As I matured and came to understand alcoholism, mental health, and trauma, I realized I did grow up in a home that was greatly impacted by generations of alcoholism and trauma; it just didn't show up in the form of one of my parents drinking themselves to death. While my mom never drank, I do believe that most of her parenting downfalls and emotional challenges were the result of being raised by two unavailable, chaotic, and mentally ill parents.

My mom recalls being witness to several of her own mother's suicide attempts, secret affairs, and wildly unrecognizable behaviors when she drank. There was a time when her dad moved out and neither parent made my mom and her brother aware of the change in their family for six months; she quickly learned that her needs weren't important to either of her parents. Both of her parents remarried, and my mom stated that because of her loving stepparents and grandparents, her childhood became a little more tolerable.

My step-grandfather was a larger-than-life man who loved my grandma wholeheartedly through decades of relapse, mental health crises, and chaos. He too was an alcoholic, meeting my grandmother in detox. They were married within months of leaving treatment. Contrary to my grandma's lifelong relationship with alcohol, my step-grandfather was sober until the day he died. My mom tried to protect my brother and me from her parents' drama throughout our childhood; Christmases were sometimes cancelled and visits to their house "changed" last minute.

Despite the separation at times, my grandma and I had a very close bond. She became my most favorite person in my family. In my younger years, she would babysit me once a week during a long stretch of her sobriety. As I grew into a teenager, we would go on shopping trips, share cigarettes out on her patio, and talk about life. When I was sixteen, after a long cocaine and alcohol binge and a chaotic breakup, I took a greyhound bus two and a half hours away to spend the weekend with her. While I assume she was in the dark about the seriousness of my addiction, she was a safe place for me to land. We were kindred spirits. However, I started to notice the difference in her eyes when she was sober and when she wasn't. Her drinking always worried me; it was like I could see and feel her pain. Once alcohol entered either of us, we displayed very similar "flip the switch" behaviors. We could both balance Dr. Jekyll and Mr. Hyde until we took too much in—then we were gone.

My dad's parents both drank daily, and from my perspective, this greatly limited in their ability to live a life outside of their narrow world. In the earlier years of my dad's childhood, he described his home as loving. He and his sisters were all born within twenty-eight months of one another and grew up very close. My paternal grandfather was a hardworking man and started his own business once they moved from Manitoba to Alberta.

As he started to work outside of the home more, his drinking increased. According to my dad, his father was a quiet man when it came to discussing difficult topics and often retreated to his room at the start of an argument or confrontation. His mother's drinking increased as her kids grew into their teen years, partially due to infidelity within the marriage and other strains in the family system. My dad and his sisters all excelled in sports, winning several awards throughout their high school years. My dad's youngest sister started to drink problematically at a very young age and has battled alcoholism her entire life. My dad, too, had his struggles with alcohol, especially after the death of his dad from cancer and the following few years during my parents' separation.

A NEW KIND OF NUMB

I started attending parties that launched me into experiences I wasn't consciously seeking but soon adapted to. The exchange of sexual favors for alcohol and drugs started around age fourteen or fifteen. At the time, I truly didn't realize the impact that these behaviors would have on my self-esteem and the fundamental belief of the role that men played in my life.

There was an understanding among my group of friends that boys my age were not able to provide us with the things we needed, mainly drugs, alcohol, and a fun party. So we strived to be part of the "older" crowd, which were the kids a couple years our senior and already in high school. Dollar "bets" became a common practice between the older guys about us younger girls; they included which one of us would let them finger bang, who would give a blowjob, and who would go "all the way."

Quietly retreating from a random bedroom was always a shameful experience. Typically the guy friends would hoot and holler, and us girls would keep our head down, eyes averted, and move toward the closest cigarette and alcoholic drink. Despite these experiences being shameful in nature and often embarrassing because of the public knowledge of what took place, they also secured a spot in the social hierarchy that I thrived to be a part of.

A lot of bad things happened to my friends too. We would maybe mention the events to one another in a drunken emotional episode but quickly move on. There have been several times where I have had a distaste in my mouth for certain people in my past only to be reminded of what they did to me at a party. I admittedly denied ever being taken advantage of or raped until I was well into my twenties; I truly thought that many of the things that happened were just "normal" parts of teenage life.

The parties we attended became more "mature" and more dangerous. The men become older, and the drugs were offered more often. By age fifteen, cocaine and ecstasy were part of my weekly life. At first, they were reserved for weekends, but eventually, I progressed to using almost nightly. My friends and I would drive around, drinking and using cocaine in the car while we blasted Nirvana or other music that made us feel something. These albums became our anthem. Like the rockstars blaring through our speakers, we, too, were seeking numbness, distance, and blackout from our wounds and emotions.

The fun party nights started to turn into distressing middle-of-the-night cravings for more cocaine. I started to experience paranoia and insufferable anxiety, which I would drown with alcohol or downers. I had brief moments of wanting to stop using drugs as a young teenager; I even ended up in an AA meeting with my mom's closest friend, but I rolled my eyes at the mention of God and long-term sobriety. I scoffed at the idea that the older men in the rooms of AA understood anything about me or about my relationship with substances. I mustered up the patience to stick around for the one-hour meeting, chain smoking in the small, rundown upstairs room of the old, rickety building. I now know that the woman sitting with me that day understood the pain of addiction and dysfunction. I saw it in her eyes and heard it in her stories, but I was nowhere near ready to admit that.

My boyfriend at the time had just turned twenty-one. I was freshly sixteen. He lived with five other men, all who loved to party and seemingly welcomed us younger girls with open arms. At the time, I certainly did not understand the significance of the age difference between us and them. Their home was filthy; dishes always filling the sink, empty beer cans and cigarette butts galore, the couches stained—quite opposite of everything I was used to at home. My friends and I started sneaking away from high school at our lunch period to go back to the party houses. We rarely attended a full day of class and often missed days at a time. I had become skilled at forging my parents' signature or answering the house phone prior to my parents arriving home to get the message from the school that I had missed again.

When we were partying and the clock started to trend into the middle of the night, my friends and I would frantically look for a place to sleep since we were all too intoxicated to get into a car. Wherever we slept, strangers' coats became my pillows, and I would consciously choose a room with another girl sleeping in it to avoid "what could happen."

My best friends and I often told our parents we were at the others' house, and after a while, it felt like no one bothered to check anymore. They tried all the "right" parenting tactics, including involving the police because I was a runaway in perceived danger. That attempt brought me home for one night. While my days were filled with scrounging for change to buy cigarettes, alcohol, and drugs or developing the next lie for the school principal to explain why I missed school again, I started to recognize some of the emotional pain I was in.

THE DARK DESCENT

A darkness was growing inside of me, and eventually it was too big to keep ignoring. On the outside, it looked like I was trying to escape my life at home when my desire really was to escape my innermost self. I started to despise who I was, what it felt like in my body, and what I saw when I looked in the mirror.

I had no idea how to communicate any of this.

To my parents.

To my friends.

To a therapist.

Even to myself.

It felt like I was losing my mind.

I started experiencing a sense of dissociation and dysmorphia. It wasn't uncommon for me to perceive my hands and head as different sizes or feel like they were floating away from my body. I would freeze in a dream state and watch my surroundings from somewhere above my head. I would give my head a literal shake, thinking that would help whatever was happening stop. In other scenarios, I desperately tried to grasp on to something around me that made me feel like I was "normal."

The voices in my head increased in frequency and happened often enough that I couldn't ignore their existence anymore. I never told a soul what was happening in my mind because I would do whatever I could to deny it. The noises from the TV seemed to come through a megaphone, or my own voice would seem far away as I spoke, like it didn't belong to me. I felt completely out of control and confused. Why did it feel like there were multiple versions of myself talking at once? Why did I feel disconnected from my physical body and my surroundings? Was I losing my mind?

When I smoked marijuana, these symptoms worsened, but when I drank, they quieted. Alcohol was solidified again as my best friend. I think most people around me knew I wasn't okay. Subtle looks of concern would flash across their face, or they would encourage me to go to bed.

If I was hungover enough or deeply heartbroken, I would go to either my mom's or dad's house. There were luxury comforts such as usable couches, a clean shower, a smokeless home, and a fridge full of food rather than beer and a random carton of eggs; but there weren't people.

Being left alone was a catch-22. The wild teenager part of me craved the freedom, but the lonely and vulnerable child in me wanted and needed connection with my parents. My brother and I split time between my mom's and dad's houses on a rotating schedule where we packed up and moved our stuff every two weeks. With time, my habit of stealing money and other forms of dishonesty caused my family to not trust me. I wasn't allowed to be in either home without anyone there. I was a tyrant in my homes. No one could stand being around me. The tension between my parents, my brother, and me was palpable. I often pushed my behavior to the absolute limit just to confirm what I felt: I wasn't wanted at home.

One day, after I finished screaming more heinous things at my mom, she looked me dead in the eye and said, "Sometimes it is really hard to be your mother."

My stomach leapt into my throat, and in my heart, I knew this was true. The room started spinning, and I unloaded more verbal assaults on her and left. I recall being gone for a few days after that blowup. I don't know who my running away punished more, myself or my parents. Years later, they recount the sleepless nights they had when I was out at all hours of the night or didn't come home for days, the ache in their heart at not knowing where I was. And then there was, of course, their fear and anticipation of who I was becoming.

A KNOCK AT THE DOOR

The summer before I turned sixteen, my friends and I went camping for a few days at the base of the Rocky Mountains in Alberta. There was a music festival in the nearby small town that we would attend, and then we planned to, somehow, make it back to our campsite while intoxicated to continue the drinking and getting high. The dangers of drinking and driving didn't often cross our mind; we mostly looked for the person who was "sober" enough to get behind the wheel. We secured ourselves with the false security of youthful invincibility when we were all together, including the older boyfriends who pretended to "take care of us."

We miraculously made it back to camp after hours of partying at the festival. My boyfriend at the time had an old dark-blue van with chipped paint and peeling ceiling carpet, and as soon as we pulled into our site in the early hours of the morning, I crawled into the back, exhausted and desperate for a few hours of sleep. Two guys from our group had other plans and tried to drive back into town. The driver was drunk and lost control, flipping the car on the road to our campsite. The passenger, who was my close friend's brother, died at the scene. I had just drifted off to sleep in the van when I was woken up by an aggressive knock on the back door while people screamed that there had been an accident.

The police quickly arrived and were all over the campsite, questioning everyone and blocking us from leaving. All of us were still intoxicated, in shock of what just unfolded.

My head was swirling, unable to fully grasp that our friend was dead on the road a few hundred feet ahead of us. We were unable to leave by car for several hours as they investigated, so we decided to walk to a nearby creek to cool off and continue to sober up.

We walked down the gravel road until we hit the yellow body bag covering him. My hands shook, my core was a melting pile of ice, and my words gathered in a painful, immovable lump in my mouth. My friend was with the group of us as we reached his brother's body bag, but it felt impossible to glance in his direction. I had no idea what to say or how to act around him. For the first time since being in my teen years, I felt too young for what we had just experienced.

Unfortunately, what should have been a wakeup call only fueled our desire for more maladaptive behaviors. I don't think any of us who were there stayed sober longer than a day.

The weekend following the accident in the woods, some friends and I were at our "second home," a rundown bungalow that housed several grown men. Some people were passed out in random chairs, on couches, and across floors; others were still awake from doing drugs all night. I was sitting on the porch, smoking a cigarette with a few others who stayed up all night snorting cocaine. The sun was rising in the sky, a signal that the day would start moving as normal for others, while I tried to sober up enough to leave and go seek solace at one of my parent's homes.

My phone rang and it was my best friend, immediately I knew something was wrong by the shake in her voice. "Chels, Justin is dead." There was no inflection in her tone.

I replayed the words in my head. *Justin is dead. Justin is dead.* Time stood still, and perplexity set in. How could one of our best friends be dead?

I was still half intoxicated and decided that the only way to help the anguish I felt bubbling in my chest was more alcohol. Someone else on the porch read my mind and started pouring shots, quickly passing them around as they gave me a worried look. My face was white, tears streamed down my face, and I couldn't find my footing as I stood up to pace. The overuse of cocaine had caused severe palpitations in my chest, increasing my desperate need to shut everything off with alcohol.

Our group of friends walked around like zombies for weeks, not knowing how to function with gaping holes in our hearts. I drank and used drugs to numb the pain that both Jer and Justin were gone and raged at how unfair losing them both was. Many of us connected through our shared sorrow, and regardless of how dysfunctional we were, we did it together, as a group of broken, angry, and lost teenagers.

Once the shock of the loss started to wear off, I started feeling the pressure of my standing in high school. I was entering my senior year and was barely skating by. While academics had always been my strong suit, I now couldn't bring myself to care about any aspect of my life that didn't involve partying. As the sun beat down on my face or the slippery ice caused me to lose my footing, the walk from the north side of town where my boyfriend lived to my high school was a walk of contemplation. I was disgusted with who I was becoming and the way I pushed my morals aside to meet the expectations of others. Aspects of me, however, continued to crave the escape from myself that I experienced with substances and older men.

EVERYTHING AND NOTHING

In March of 2005, two months before my high school graduation, my dad called me and said that we needed to meet at his house for an urgent matter. Thoughts of everything I could have done wrong recently flooded my mind, and my hands shook with anxiety as I disconnected the call. I dreaded whatever new consequence he had for my behavior or yet another discussion of how disappointed he was in me.

My brother and I arrived at my dad's house at the same time. We sat around the oval kitchen table as our dad shared the news: our maternal grandmother had died in her sleep the night before, with a bottle of alcohol and pills next to her. My brother let out a desperate sound of confusion and shock, but I remained silent.

I was devastated. Just a few days earlier, I had been smoking in my mom's garage while she packed for her trip to Costa Rica when the phone rang. It was my grandma, and she was very drunk, speaking nonsense. Hearing her voice full of so much hopelessness and despair left me feeling angry; it was not my job to support her like this. I annoyedly opened the door to the house and shouted for my mom. As she entered the garage, I quickly handed her the phone while mouthing the words, "She's really drunk."

I had been moderately aware of my grandma's alcoholism and mental health struggles, and unfortunately, as mine increased, my understanding of hers grew. Despite her dysfunction, she was often my confidant, the adult I felt least judged by and one of the people I called when life felt too hard.

I slowly came back to reality in my dad's kitchen, and we robotically discussed logistics. Did my mom know? How quickly could she get home from Costa Rica?

The heartbreak surrounding my grandma's death was felt by everyone in my family, especially her husband, who was dying of cancer at the time of her death and desperately needed his wife during his final days. We held her service at his hospice center. It was small but intimate, slightly convoluted by whispers of the cause of death and intoxicated family members in attendance. Exactly one week later, my grandpa passed away; they were together again at last.

Between the traumatic grief, constant partying, my feeble attempt at completing my senior-year coursework, and the typical chaos of teenage life, the two months after my grandma's death were a blur. I could not fully accept that she was gone. My body lived in a state of shock most of the time, sometimes shifting into complete shutdown or a hyper-fixated "go-go" version of me who could pretend that everything was okay.

It took me a long time to recognize a chronic symptom that I had been experiencing: I developed unbearable thirst. I was so ravished for fluids that I would chug water, juice, or milk, attempting to quench this unquenchable feeling. I assumed that it was caused from too much alcohol and not enough water. This explanation allowed me to brush off other, much scarier, possibilities.

I began to look sickly, way beyond the "heroin chic" aesthetic that was popular in the early 2000s. My parents often accused me of drinking alcohol even when I hadn't drunk that day. They would move closer to me, sniffing my breath, my clothes, and the air around me, trying to prove they were right. Starvation would hit and my entire body would shake. My brain felt like it was slowly losing power, and until I got a substantial amount of food in me, these symptoms would not go away. I eventually looked bad enough that my parents took me to get bloodwork done by our family doctor.

Early the next morning, as I slowly opened my eyes from a restless night's sleep, I stared at the black-and-white checkered floor in my room, blurrily trying to find the source of the wet and cold feeling in my bed. As I realized what had happened, I was overcome with confusion; the bed was soaked in my urine. I quickly removed the sheets and ran up the stairs to start the washing machine before my dad or stepmom saw me. I showered, got ready, and went to school without telling a soul what had taken place.

I was sitting in one of my last classes of high school senior year, discussing with my friends the debauchery of each "themed" party that took place that week, when the overhead speaker turned on and I was called to the principal's office. My mom was waiting for me when I arrived and before I could ask what was wrong, she hurried me out of the school. As we walked, she spoke words that seemed foreign to me. I couldn't grasp the totality of her statements or what it meant regarding me. Our family doctor told my mom that

I was being diagnosed with juvenile diabetes (type 1) and that it was urgent that we go home to pack the necessities and admit me to the hospital.

All I remember from the next several days in the PICU was the sound of my dad crying in the hallway in between visitors and the noticeable fear in everyone's eyes. My mom was stoic like always and seemed disconnected, focusing on interrogating the doctors for every detail about the disease. I went into my own pretend world, convincing myself that what was happening to me wasn't serious and I would be able to carry on with my lifestyle; I even asked the doctors if I could still drink alcohol.

After I stabilized enough to drag my IV bag and insulin drip around, we were taken to a separate room with a long, dark, wooden conference table. Here, my parents and I were handed a fake piece of "body fat" and taught to inject insulin. As I sat there, I glanced down at my own stomach that was depleted of all fat. I was dangerously thin and white as a ghost; how would I ever inject myself? The medical team reminded me that small children with less body fat than me manage to do it, so I could too.

As I sat there, watching my parents repeatedly practice with a forced look of encouragement on their faces, I floated away from myself, observing the scene like it was happening to someone else's family. Reflecting on these first few days, I was already physically and mentally a shell of a person, so being handed a life-altering diagnosis only increased my tendency to dissociate. Truthfully, all I could focus on was whether I could continue living my life like I had been, drinking and partying with my friends and boyfriend.

A few days after diagnosis, it was my high school graduation. The medical team approved me to leave the hospital so I could attend the ceremony and dinner, if my parents didn't leave my side. Pictures of me from that day show the translucent skin, emaciated figure, and undeniable fatigue in my eyes. Most people around me seemed to forget that I was close to death only a few days prior, including me. I forced a smile on my face for the pictures but collapsed internally every time my parents reminded me to check my blood sugar and go to the bathroom to inject myself with insulin. My friends would come into the bathroom stall to help me maneuver my long black silk dress to get to my stomach, which quickly became covered in small needle pricks.

When I was diagnosed, insulin pumps weren't readily available, and continuous glucose monitors had not been developed yet. I obsessively checked my blood sugar but with a different goal than staying healthy; I was determined to not allow it to drop low enough where I couldn't drink alcohol or go about my day as I wanted. I was terrified of low blood sugar and how out of control it made me feel. The patterns that I developed trying to manage my alcoholism and type 1 diabetes led me down a path of further self-destruction. I learned to master manipulating my doses of insulin and the carbs I did or didn't eat, all to ensure I could party how I wanted. I was deathly afraid of gaining weight, rhetoric from the nineties shouted in my head like I had to listen, reinforcing the belief that being stick thin was the answer to my depleted self-esteem.

In the months after my diagnosis, I continued to drink to numbness and blackout; being aware of aspects of my life felt too unbearable. I would wake up from a night out, shaking, out of breath, confused, and downright scared by what I was doing to my body. Despite my attempts to "cheat the system," due to the amount of alcohol that I would drink, my blood sugar often crashed dangerously low, which mimicked the feeling of a panic attack. Some of these low episodes involved intervention from EMS or others around me.

I was angry at my diagnosis and at the way it impacted my ability to live the way I wanted; my life was wholly interrupted. Without realizing it, I transferred some of the responsibility of taking care of myself onto others. I became enraged when my people around me didn't take action to control my blood sugar or ensure I had sugar "fast enough." All questions asked by others related to my diabetes were stupid questions; I expected everyone who loved me to know every answer without a doubt. I deeply yearned for others to be connected to my pain. I desperately wanted to be fully seen, felt, and heard felt like the most important thing in the world.

NEW START, SAME PATH

After graduation, my boyfriend and I continued our outlandish relationship for a few more months. I once even attempted to take responsibly for his DUI by jumping into the driver seat when we got pulled over while intoxicated. The cop easily saw the attempted switch and quickly and sternly sent me home. My self-worth and self-esteem continued to crumble as the cheating, fights, and chaos ensued. I was in the bars multiple times a week, getting in physical fights, drinking my weight in vodka, and eventually being the one friend who people didn't want to drink with anymore.

The conflicting thoughts I had about men were glaring. A large part of me hated them. It wasn't rare for me to be hit on and then respond with a fist to their nose. On the other hand, I continued to seek out their attention and would experience crippling tightness in my chest and a sinking feeling in my stomach if their attention went toward someone else. There were many times that I would bang on the door to my boyfriend's house and find him with someone else or hear through the grapevine that he was hooking up with an acquaintance. For some reason, I always believed his apologies and felt I was special enough to him to change his behaviors. This drawn-out hope shattered my confidence. I learned that my fears of being replaced and lied to were trustworthy, but I adamantly went against them because I desperately needed his attention.

Several months after graduation, my best friends and I had all broken up (or were in the process of breaking up) with the men we had dated throughout high school. I'm not sure how the decision was made but it was: we were going to move to Australia. I don't recall our parents' reactions or whether the idea was initially supported, but before I knew it, we all had plane tickets to escape Southern Alberta. Due to me being type 1 diabetic, obtaining a visitor visa wasn't as straightforward for me as it was for my friends. I ended up needing additional testing and clearance before I was able to enter Australia. If my memory is correct, they arrived a couple weeks ahead of me, and I ended up making the trip across the world on my own.

Upon landing in Sydney, the freedom I felt ran deep. Being in a new country allowed me to start over without the reputation I had back home, and it was much easier to lie to my parents about my substance use. On a positive note, the trip allowed me to build back up independence that I had lost in my last relationship.

My time in Australia was full of adventure. We started in Sydney and traveled up the Gold Coast, stopping in many different towns and sleeping in hostels where we met expats from around the world. We laughed, we fought, we drank too much, and we made countless memories together. While the trip was not without bumps in the road, including a cyclone and a sailing trip that almost turned deadly, the experiences we had were much different than we had back home. We weren't taken advantage of the way we were used to, and "bad" things weren't happening to us daily.

After twelve weeks abroad, I had maxed out my credit cards, faced several severe episodes of low blood sugar due to drinking too much, and felt homesick. I decided to make the trip back home without telling anyone besides my step-mom, who was helping me surprise my parents. I was in the middle of the Sydney airport, waiting to board my flight, when the walls around me started to spin. After checking my blood sugar and seeing that it was low, I went to buy some juice at a convenience store. Unbeknownst to me, that same morning my dad had shut off my credit card due to my spending habits, so my transaction declined. My heart raced as I flagged down a security guard and frantically asked for candy or some form of sugar before I passed out. The look of concern and disappointment on his face reminded me of how reckless I was being with my health. Unfortunately, the fear that I felt that day did little to improve my focus and dedication to becoming a more disciplined diabetic.

My surprise to my parents went off without a hitch, and they both cried happy tears to see me home. Upon my return, I quite literally sprinted back to the party scene. The friends I went to Australia with didn't come back until four months and twelve months after our original arrival. Thankfully, I had many friends still left in Lethbridge. We often went to a different bar for every night of the week, besides one night that was for "rest." My hangovers were severe, and I was miserable; the only time I smiled and felt anything at all was when I was drunk. To balance the negative trajectory I was on, I enrolled in community college. There were still parts of me that wanted to excel in life and make something of myself. This part of me was disconnected from the trauma, my mental health, and any true acceptance that I was an alcoholic. I chose psychology as my major and proudly told people when they asked, oblivious to the contradictions in the way I lived my life.

him

RETURN

Bartending provided me with an endless supply of alcohol and quick, easy money. My drunkenness, dishevelment, and chaotic life was never questioned in that environment either. My coworkers and I basked in each other's lifestyles, often encouraging drinking to excess during and after work.

I was cleaning beer glasses in the bar and tidying up after the post-work rush when a man entered the bar with an air of confidence, sat down, and ordered a drink. The moment my eyes met his, my stomach dropped, and I flashed back to a time when I was fifteen years old.

My friend and I were invited to a seedy motel room by someone she knew who supplied her with drugs. As I entered the motel room, the door clicked behind me, and I quickly surveilled my surroundings. The room was filled with cigarette smoke, alcohol bottles, and a variety of illegal drugs. While it was wildly different from my home life, it was similar enough to the party houses I frequented to feel familiar. But I still felt uneasy. I stood there, uncomfortable, and unsure as anxiety flowed through my body. I reluctantly found a narrow slice of empty bed and took a seat. I distinctly remember feeling like a child, smaller and weaker than everyone else around me, but I kept on a brave and indifferent expression on my face.

The man at the bar was the man in my memory. He sat on the bed, holding a pipe as he showed my friend and I how to smoke meth. He spoke softly but sternly, grooming us to feel safe in a situation that was anything but. "I think it's so hot when girls smoke meth," he said. I didn't know how to respond besides drinking from the glass that another man had given me. I suddenly wanted to leave but was unsure if I would be allowed to.

This predatory behavior felt significantly more dangerous than any encounters I'd had previously. However, I had learned from past experiences that even if I didn't want a part in what was happening around me, there was often no choice. "Going along with it" was the best way to eventually escape.

I quickly reoriented myself in the present, pouring the drink that the man had ordered, vibrating with conflicting unease and excitement. Just as my memory faded, he reminded me that we had met years before. He went on to explain how he was just released from prison after serving five years for drug trafficking charges. There was no remorse in his voice. Instead, he elaborated through a series of sob stories about not being able to see his children due to the "evilness" of his ex-wife and the torture he experienced while locked up. We discussed the friends we still had in common and what he had missed in his many years away.

He was enduring, charming, and seemingly curious about who I was.

The intensity surrounding him did not feel scary enough to run away. Instead, it provided me with an unhealthy thrill. There were many significant moments in the early years of re-meeting him that I went against my internal alarm bells. Things moved quickly between us despite him simultaneously sleeping with one of my coworkers, which caused months of chaos in our "relationship." Deep down, I knew I should have run far away from him, but the high from his charm and attention outweighed any logic.

The intensity of his personality, at times smothering, was a very effective way to pave the belief that I was important to him. He seemed obsessed with me, but he also obviously and repeatedly betrayed the connection I thought we had. The constant confusion led to me building tolerance for emotional rollercoasters and an eventual inability to trust my own sanity.

My drug use quickly picked up in the beginning of our relationship. I went right back to using cocaine daily and hanging out with people who were much more dangerous than those in my previous party years. Almost everyone around me were drug dealers and/or current victims of significant abuse and domestic violence, and many were very violent individuals. My ability to be on high alert to my surroundings really came in handy during this time. From the moment I entered a relationship with him, my nervous system never hung out in a stable zone. Throughout the following years, I lost all comprehension of what safety was. This undertone of lack of safety stuck with me for many years. I found myself questioning why I felt to scared all the time, oblivious to the traumas my body held onto.

Despite my instability in many areas, I had much more than he did: enrollment in college, a job, and a safe-enough living arrangement. He was living in a halfway house, jobless, on parole, and had minimal contact with his children. His narrative of victimhood mixed with dangerousness attracted me, partially because I was a psychology major in school and because I had the "traumatized blueprint" already. His chaos was familiar to me.

I remained fairly disconnected to the impact his behavior had on me. I even wrote a paper for my forensic psychology class, focusing on antisocial behavior, that was loosely based on him. I got an A in the paper without anyone finding out it was about a man I shared a bed with at night. I had heard many horror stories of who he was through the grapevine, but I could not align that supposed villain with how elated he made me feel most days.

The abuse started off subtle but was calculated, which made it nearly impossible for me to identify and describe to others. The stark differences in what he said and what he did created such a fog of confusion that differentiating the truth from the false became impossible. The inappropriate sexual behaviors toward myself and friends of mine were the initial warning signs. I was naïve to the fact that what he did wasn't out of passion but control and sadism.

Initially, he framed much of his abuse as him teaching me about my body, satisfying his uncontrollable desires, and wanting to please me. He insisted that I was worth bragging about through pictures, inappropriate oversharing, and hidden video cameras. It became impossible for me to use my voice as a form of self-protection unless I was intoxicated, which often led to drag-out fights that I eventually decided weren't worth it.

At the one-year mark of our relationship, we had broken up too many times to count; it always ended with both of us begging for each other back and a swift transition back to chaos and drug use. Deep down, I asked myself why I went back so many times. It wasn't that I wanted to. I felt like I had no choice. I was propelled by an intense cycle that I could not explain. Those of you who have been in relationships plagued by domestic violence and addiction may understand. He had managed to create a trauma bond quickly. He knew how to make me feel on top of the world while dangerously dragging me to my lowest point. I was quickly programmed to the belief that everything was my fault and that I would have to beg for forgiveness for the harm that he caused me.

ANARCHY

I was in the living room of a friend's house whose basement we often inhabited; I had a clear vision of *him* down the hall in another room using drugs. I watched him smoke something from a pipe. In that moment I needed whatever that was he had. I frantically wanted to feel a high so strong that it brought me to my knees.

The intensity of smoking crack cocaine was my new adventure and obsession. Snorting cocaine and drinking alcohol didn't quite quench the desire for complete oblivion any longer. I began to crave a drug in a way that I never had before; I would eventually do anything for more crack.

He used me a lot as bait to connect with dealers he had owed money to. Most of the time it worked, and they didn't question answering the phone for a young woman. But this new role of mine came with a lot of accusatory statements from him as well as false information spreading to my friends that I continually cheat on him. The delusion in which he lived soon became my delusion. I started to forget my truth and became confused at my own thoughts, feelings, and behaviors. I was forced to believe what he told me because questioning anything was not safe, emotionally or physically. He stepped out of our relationship constantly, while simultaneously accusing me of doing so; he would smell my clothes, my underwear, and my body to ensure I wasn't lying to him.

The oblivion of my active addiction is hard to recount at times because of the parallel lives I lived. I often attempted to appear "normal" and functioning. We would attend his family events, take his children for a few days, and occasionally see my friends and family. As I slowly met extended members of his family, I started to see a lot of generational dysfunction and trauma.

He and his cousins recounted awful stories of "gang banging" women together that made my stomach turn. The sexual horrors seemed to be a normalized behavior that they spoke about freely. His mom told me heinous experiences she had at the hands of his biological dad, which ignited an undeniable truth; he was just like his father.

There were many times that his brothers and others who knew him well encouraged me to leave. I held a sense of responsibility to his kids as a reason to stay, convincing myself that I was the most stable "parental" figure they had.

I started to notice concerning behaviors such as parentification and mature topics being discussed with them that were persuasive enough for them to idolize their father despite his complete lack of caregiving. He began to make inappropriate remarks and gestures toward young girls in our life and displayed an uncomfortable level of physical affection. Just like most of his other behaviors, I tucked them away deep inside because the reality around me could not possibly be true.

Through his own convincing, manipulative, and dangerous tactics, I had been pressured into adopting his radically different ways of living than my own. Granted, severe drug addiction and alcoholism clouded my perception of myself and others. I can self-assuredly conclude that my mind and soul began to change into someone I did not recognize.

To some people, he was the most helpful person on the planet, always ready to lend a hand in a project involving physical labor. The mask he wore around others resulted in a lot of people not believing how awful he was to me, even after our eventual breakup. There were some people throughout the years who came close—mostly other men who did stand up for me regarding the physical violence, but they still accepted the display of my naked body at his direction with no problem.

At times, the women in our circle of drug addicts and alcoholics seemed jealous of the intensity his affection and obsession with me. I soon began to realize it was because he offered them the same thing when I wasn't around. The physical intimidation and violence that he exhibited was an effective tool to keep me quiet and fearful of what could happen next if I didn't obey. Unfortunately, I was mouthy and sometimes violent when I was intoxicated, which, according to him, resulted in "legitimate" reasons to hurt me.

The black eyes became more frequent, which led to me creating stories to cover up what was happening. I remember countless excuses: "I hit my eye on the door frame," "I hit it on the coffee table," or "I'm not sure what happened last night; I woke up like this." My best friends didn't believe a word I said regarding my safety, my drug use, or where I disappeared to for weeks at a time. The lies would just spill out of my mouth with no thought behind them. They were rightfully concerned and despised my relationship with him. Despite the growing evidence against him, there was a part of me that felt confused and in disbelief that he behaved this way toward me.

He thrived on my vulnerable state. He used it as a launching pad to build me back up after a series of actions that ripped away my safety, self-worth, and autonomy. When I did choose to spend time with the people who truly loved me, I immediately switched into a different version of myself, one that I recognized.

LOSS OF SELF

Crack houses involve a different level of disgust that I had not yet been exposed to. The overall risk of becoming a victim at any moment was constant; I am still shocked at the degree to which people were willing or driven to bend their morals for another hit. I had been around a lot of debauchery in the past but could explain most of it by over toxication on alcohol and other party substances, but these occurrences were different. The only way I could stand to be around or involved in these situations was to be so high that nothing about me felt real.

I have quick images in my mind of fights breaking out and blood splattering on the walls and ceilings. I see flashes of violent behavior toward outsiders of the "group." I remember one moment where he and another dangerous felon kidnapped a taxi driver. While the physical violence around me was frequent, the underlying tone of sexual violence and lack of choice lingered like a rotten smell in the air; pornography was always on the TV, men were often masturbating or making suggestive sexual advances and misogynistic comments toward the women, and there was a constant threat that anything could and would happen if you let your guard down at the wrong moment.

I would never use crack without him due to what would happen to me if I did. In our own sick, twisted way, it was the time we "connected." We rarely fought while using crack heavily. I was so deep in a state of fawning to his every desire and demand that I didn't have the strength to fight back. When the drugs ran out and the alcohol wore off, we were stuck with intense cravings, high levels of paranoia, and distrust toward one another, resulting in violent and scary fights. In the wee hours of the morning or late in the next day, I would come to, sweating, shaking, and out of breath, my hair often stuck to my face, my pupils the size of black saucers; in these moments, I had no clue who I had become.

This intense dynamic changed my brain chemistry. I was consistently oscillating between fight, flight, fawn, freeze, and shutdown. Unfortunately, years of these patterns led me to "know" how to play the game that was necessary for survival. I had become so desensitized to his behaviors and abuse that my mind and body had no idea how to function without it. A hovering sense of impending doom haunted me every morning until I knew what version of him I would be interacting with that day.

Every time I opened my eyes, arrived home, or answered a phone call, I would sense how I needed to adjust to his moods, wants, and desires. Switching states was completely automatic; my mind and body knew what I needed to survive another day in a relationship with him. There would be brief moments of recognizing that I was living a completely split life. I would get flashes of who I was the day or night before, and I would shudder, shocked at who I could become in a split second.

He grew bolder in his cheating. Everyone knew what he was doing to me, and behind my back, he often brought sex workers and other women to the house we shared while I wasn't home. He started to dangle these other women in my face, sending me pictures of them together, often naked, and screenshots of messages between them. I had occasional waves of apathy toward his cheating because a part of me wanted him to find a new victim in hopes of leaving me alone, but the obsessiveness I still had with him often won.

Some days, I went into full panic mode, trying to find out where he was, who he was with, and how I could intervene on the cheating. The delusion that my feelings had power over him would overtake my behaviors and lead to complete humiliation. There were many times when I would find him completely unphased by the dynamics of our relationship and others. Other times, he would be completely devastated at the thought of losing me. I never knew which one I was going to get.

One night, a friend of his hinted that he had other women over at his house. I drove there quickly with the intent of "catching him" and informing the other woman what a bad person he was. When I arrived, I quickly ran into the house, but it was empty. There was evidence of drug use and drinking, but it appeared people had left in a hurry. As I looked around the house, I heard noise from downstairs and found a roommate of his still there. He quickly bounded up the stairs, full of intensity and anger in his eyes.

Historically, this roommate had never been abusive toward me, but tonight was different. He was in an absolute rage, a seeming psychosis due to being awake for days on crack and other substances. An argument began between the two of us about something trivial, and next thing I knew, he was ripping out every appliance in the kitchen and throwing them at me. The basement stairs were closer than an exit, so I bolted down them and ran into the bathroom, slamming the door. The coffee maker, microwave, and other smaller appliances came hurling down the stairs after me. I did something then I thought I would never do: I called the police.

When the commotion stopped and police sirens wailed from down the street, I carefully stepped from the bathroom and made my way upstairs. The refrigerator was halfway across the kitchen, ripped from the outlet in the wall. Other kitchen items were thrown about like a tornado had passed through. The roommate had fled by the time the police arrived, and I was left by myself in a house with illegal weapons, drugs, and who knew what else hiding in the closets.

Thankfully, I was sober that evening, and the police believed my narration of events and that I did not live there. However, their help stopped there. Eventually, I was free to go and walked to my car, only to be met with a shattered windshield. The police suggested I call a cab before they left.

A TIPPING POINT

As the months went on, the chaos continued, and the disturbing events multiplied. It became second nature to separate myself from the experiences for me to continue on participating in society. Living life through two different lenses became new state of being it was my new normal and I wasn't even aware at the time. The lies and behaviors felt like they belonged to a different version of myself, which made being honest to those around me feel completely out of reach. It was like I was watching the different versions of myself live a life I did not recognize.

Throughout these years in my life, I completed a college associate degree and began university. An internal switch would flip, and I could put on my studious hat and engage in my neuropsychology and criminology classes. But eventually, my ability to write exams and pass classes grew nonexistent. I could no longer keep it together for work and eventually quit my job. Visits with friends and family became infrequent, and my health was deteriorating quickly.

My eyes met the carpet as I crawled along the carpeted floor in my dad's basement, trying to reach the bathroom while I puked up a black substance. A few days prior, I had found out I was pregnant. I was devastated when I saw the "pregnant" flash on the stick. Despite the devastation I felt at the thought of being pregnant with his baby, I was scared about what was taking place within my body. On top of being newly pregnant, I was detoxing and seriously sick with the swine flu. I don't recall the drive to the hospital with my dad, but I came to in the triage room as they checked my temperature while I nodded in and out of awareness. I briefly heard the words "not sure if she will make it."

The beeping of the hospital machines woke me up. Glancing around the room, I saw my mom and dad, fully covered in protective gear to prevent the spread of the virus. The sterileness of the room scared me. The blank looks on everyone's faces made my stomach churn. And yet all I thought about was getting out of there to smoke a cigarette and use a substance.

I spent several long days in the hospital. Recovering from diabetic ketoacidosis and the swine flu virus was no easy task on my body. There were no visitors allowed, besides the hospital minister who I quickly asked to leave. Having someone offering to pray for me sent me into a rage. How would their meaningless pleas to a God I did not believe in change my life circumstances? The room phone rang; it was a nurse from the diabetes pregnancy team. She asked what I needed from them, and I stated, "Nothing. I am not keeping the baby."

She responded with, "Bless your heart, dear." I hung up immediately.

I miscarried shortly after.

Despite my recent health scares, the management of my type 1 diabetes continued to be on the back burner; sometimes it was completely out of sight. I often ended up back in the hospital to receive fluids to flush out the extra sugar and toxins that had built up in my body. I rarely took my insulin or ate. I sustained myself on orange juice to prevent lows and ensure that I could continue drinking and using drugs.

I sat in the ER one day, separated by a curtain from the other patients. I was hooked up to bags of fluids via an IV in my hand. The doctor came to see me. He looked me in the eye and said, "You must change your lifestyle, or you will die." For a flash of a second, I knew deep down that he was right. Despite the way I treated my body, I didn't want to die, but I struggled immensely at the thought of living a life without substances because that meant living without *him*.

The level of carelessness I had regarding my health when I was actively using drugs not only shocks me but saddens me for what my future held and the health complications I would eventually face.

IN BETWEEN

Several months before the relationship ended, I started to experience momentary glimpses of wanting to leave. At one point, I moved out and stayed with a woman I worked with in an apartment that was three blocks from my house with him. The dynamics were confusing at this time. The space and separation from him provided me with small moments of safety but also increased my obsessiveness over what he was doing behind my back. I would manage to put together a couple days clean from drugs but rarely alcohol; that was more socially acceptable amongst all people in my life even though I rarely drank normally.

One night, as I entered my room after a long day of work at a new restaurant job, I saw my curtains blowing in the wind. My window was wide open with a broken screen. I knew he had scaled the building and broken in to check if I was home and who I was with. From an objective standpoint, I was frightened by the intrusion, but as I personalized his actions, a part of me felt vindicated that he cared about me enough to check on me.

I started to connect with drug dealers on my own without him knowing, and my addiction deepened. The desperation I felt to not be aware of my own life was overpowering. Our relationship was at the peak of its dysfunction. Sexual abuse and coercion made up the bulk of our time together, whether through him pressuring me to show myself to other men in person or on video, us entertaining his sick and twisted obsessions, or him demanding me to perform the way the porn stars did on the films he constantly had playing.

These events required me to separate completely from myself. There was no way this could be happening to me. My brain did an impressive job—it allowed me to watch what was happening like it was a movie, and when it was over, I could turn the movie off. The level of disgust and shame I felt when I connected back to myself was often too much for me to acknowledge, let alone process, so I kept those feelings hidden away, far away from any visible version of myself.

Despite the despairing want for my life to change, my obsession to get high was too powerful, and I continued for another several weeks. On one of my late-night runs to get drugs, tears streamed down my face as I gripped my bag of crack. I rolled down the car window and held the bag of drugs out the window, daring myself to let it fly into the wind. In that moment, I was certain that I couldn't keep living the way I was, but I had zero notion on how to live sober. The loneliness that most addicts experience while in active addiction came rushing into my body. Although I still had people who would help me if I asked, the overwhelming humiliation of who I had become stopped me from reaching out.

I was under the assumption that my best friends pushed me away because they were "sick of me" and couldn't handle me anymore. But the truth was that they hated him and were heartbroken as they watched me slowly lose my life. A part of me wanted my parents to rescue me. I needed them to pluck me out of the house and lock me away from him. Over the years, most people in my life had received countless panicked phone calls asking to come pick me up, middle-of-the-night drunken messages, pleas for them to help me pack up my stuff, but these cries were always followed up with endless excuses from me about why I wouldn't leave for good.

When I started to live in the apartment down the street from our house, I eventually adjusted to short moments without contact to him. I can now see that period as a vital step toward building tolerance to leave him permanently. The time I spent apart from him varied; days could go by without me seeing him, but the abusive cycle kept taking me back. I felt in homeostasis when we were together, even if it was explosive and chaotic. This relationship took what I had left of self-agency and contorted it into what I needed to survive the power struggle of domestic violence. Without this protective aspect of myself, the self-hatred would have killed me.

There were moments where I could recognize the sickness of our relationship, but those were fleeting and often felt like they were wiped away from my mind. I once read that seeking answers from an abuser is like chasing the snake who bit you, demanding to know why. I desperately wanted answers for why he tortured me in the ways that he did, but over time I knew, no "answer" would suffice because the "why" didn't really matter.

Sometime in early 2010, there was a knock on my apartment door. When I opened it, I saw my divorced parents standing there together. I reluctantly let them in. I had recently made it back to my apartment after being awake for over forty-eight hours with him. I was distraught and exhausted. It took them both a few minutes to sit down. My dad paced, his eyes red from crying. My mom took in my appearance with shock and looked terrified at what she might hear come out of my mouth. I was curled on the couch, shut down. I had no fight left in me.

For the previous several weeks, I had been committing bank fraud. I would deposit fake checks into the bank machine and pull out the "funds." I was typically able to gather enough money to put back into my account before the check "cleared" with the bank, but this last time, I did not. The bank had called my dad, concerned about the actions I had taken on my account, and so he and my mom were here to check up on me. I attempted to create a measly lie, but unfortunately, I'd been caught on camera in the bank drive thru at all hours of the night writing blank checks to cash for imagined money.

Eventually, I collapsed into a ball of anguish under the gentle but stern concern of my parents. I don't remember saying a lot, just crying with hopelessness. I had run out of steam. I was sick of the lying; the manipulation, the loneliness, the guilt, and the shame were too much to carry anymore.

A GLIMPSE OF SAFETY

Several weeks prior to my escape, my dad had left a piece of writing for me to read when I was ready. It was his perspective on watching his daughter slowly die. I picked up the journal from him, set it on the passenger seat in my red Honda Accord, and started the drive to my apartment. I was emotionally broken and physically sick, just coming down from a few days' binge of drugs and abuse.

I pulled over on the side of the road, lit a cigarette, and then started reading the journal. The words on the page quickly became wet with my tears. The little girl inside of me was confused and satisfied. Growing up, my dad was not prone to expressing his feelings, and parts of me did not know how to respond to what I was reading.

While I never once questioned my dad's love for me, I did question how I felt when we would discuss hard things or his emotional response to me. As I read what he wrote, l felt seen in a way I desperately needed and wanted from my parents the past several years. He recognized how sick I was in my withering physical body and the complete vacancy in my eyes.

I had never once stopped to think how my addiction and lifestyle had been impacting my parents at an emotional level. I saw their frustration, their angry outbursts in response to my lying and outright intolerable behaviors, but I don't recall ever seeing an emotive expression from either of them. As I read my dad's heart on paper, he stated how powerless he felt while watching me slowly die.

I never questioned the words my dad wrote down in that journal, but I did struggle to understand what took my family so long to confront me. My behavior and life had been out of control for several years, and now, I was fighting a chronic illness that felt invisible to most people in my life. I desperately needed someone to take control of it for me.

I had always remained in some sort of contact with my family, through all the turbulence. There may have been several days in between contact, but I always let them know if I was safe or not. Throughout my relationship with *him*, my contact with my parents, brother, and friends lessened dramatically. They wouldn't see me for longer periods of time, and I started missing birthdays, events, and some holidays.

There was a deep ache in my stomach, a silent plea for the people I loved to see the way I was living and come save me.

Sometime in early 2010, I was driving down the road toward my mom's condo when she called me to remind me that it was the five-year anniversary of my grandma's death. The call was seemingly intended to make a shared emotional connection that had been missing for years. A sudden urgency crashed through my chest, and I immediately knew I needed to ask for help. The words escaped my mouth without much thought: "I need to go to treatment."

It was silent on the other end for what felt like minutes. Eventually, after a wary "okay," my mom instructed me to go upstairs into her room and pick up the notebook on top of her dresser. She had compiled a list of possible treatment centers for me.

Despite the urgency that I felt that day to escape the relationship and get off drugs and alcohol, I did what most addicted people do: I stalled the process. I had swayed those around me to stay and let me finish the spring semester of university despite my complete inability to remain clean and sober. My ability to live starkly different versions of my own life was on full display.

During the last few weeks before I entered treatment, I had consciously made the decision that my problems were solely *him* and drugs. I desperately wanted to hold on to my ability to drink alcohol because it felt more tolerable than a life without any substances. There were several nights that I went out with my friends who didn't use drugs, trying to prove to myself and them that my problem wasn't alcohol at all.

During these times of my denial, I drank too much, reacted angrily to those around me, desperately sought attention from him, and made other reckless decisions. The nights I was without him may have looked a little different because my surroundings were "safer," but the drowning of my internal pain was the same.

I was behind the wheel of my car, racing from the small town his parents lived in back to the city because we had found money for drugs and wanted one last "run" before I left. The back-and-forth screaming had already started as we sped down the highway, filled with anticipation and angst for our next fix of crack. I don't recall the context of our fight, but I have a flash of me screaming in his face, "I don't love you!"

He grabbed the wheel of the car quickly and aggressively, turning it so quickly, I was sure we were going to flip.

Seconds later, without explanation, we were safely on the side of the road. My stomach was in my throat and my heart palpating outside of my chest. I could not wait to escape him that night; his energy smothered to the point of suffocation. Despite my intrinsic need to be rid of him, we spent all night together using drugs. I spent much of the time floating next to my body, watching myself engage in actions I desperately did not want to.

There was no single moment when I suddenly became brave enough to live. There was only exhaustion—a bone-deep weariness that made staying sick harder than trying something new.

PART THREE

recovery

THE FIRST FLICKER OF LIGHT

As my mom and I drove up the switchbacks on the mountain side, I stared at the desert landscape that was so foreign to me. The day prior, we had flown from Calgary to Phoenix, Arizona, and settled into my mom and step-dad's winter home for the evening. I'd savored my last glass of wine at dinner.

The next morning, we got in the car and started the two hour drive to Prescott where the rehab facility was. I had eventually picked A Soberway Home from my mom's journal of notes, mostly due to the pool that was in the backyard of the seeming vacation home.

On the drive, we spoke about trivial things, staying away from the topic that flooded our minds. I stared out the window for the car ride, blank and numb and overwhelmed. Occasionally, I would realize that I was about to be away from everything and everyone familiar, including substances, causing an apple-sized lump to grow in my throat.

Upon arriving at the building where treatment took place, the buzz rang through the milieu that the "crack addict" from Canada was finally arriving. I guess they had been waiting for me for weeks. The building was on a small hill connected to a church. I was not a religious person, and neither were my parents. The only time we attended church was for a wedding or funeral. Despite the "Oprah show" approval and advertisement of the treatment center on national TV, the grounds were not fancy, and the building was unimpressive.

The intake coordinator tried to relate to me by sharing about his personal addiction and how his life was saved through treatment and AA. I picked my cuticles as they asked me questions about my history. I reported no childhood trauma, moderate substance use, and "bad relationship" experiences. I grossly underreported everything I had experienced, not to maliciously lie but to maintain the separation between me and my reality.

After all the clients were released from therapy, we were told that everyone would be driven back to the residence. My mom and I drove there in silence.

The experience of entering that house was more than I can accurately describe. The house was modest, with several bedrooms that had been converted into shared spaces for the women. As I entered my new room, I noticed the blank walls, the mismatched bedding, and the old wooden bunkbed set. While the aesthetic wasn't appealing, the room looked good enough to get a full night's rest. As I flashed back to the seedy motels, the mattresses on the floor, and the drug dealers' homes in which I frequently slept, the unappealing visual was no big deal. I watched as my mom looked around the home with a grim look on her face, only smiling hesitantly at me when she caught me watching her. I knew what she was thinking: the setup was not what she expected, but she had no choice but to leave me. We said our goodbyes, and she was gone.

I was twenty two years old, felt like a complete child, and was completely untrusting of everyone. I was left alone in a different country with no money or any way to leave. Strangers surrounded me, and while they seemed nice enough, I had no idea how to trust anything or anyone. I had never lived with a group of strangers before. There were about a dozen women living in this home. They were all "in recovery." I didn't really know what that meant. Worst of all, I was without any of the coping skills I had come to rely upon, dangerous or not. It was a paradoxical moment crowded with both intense fear and unexplainable gratitude for escaping what I had.

I started therapy the next day. I remember sitting in my first group therapy session. I sat on the floor, back against the wall, barely able to speak. My heart raced as I looked around at the men and women who appeared friendly and engaged in conversation with one another. Substance use treatment was an entirely new experience for me, but for several of my peers, they had been in and out of treatment for years. The thought that I would be here forever freaked me out.

Everyone was talking and laughing and crying and saying things like, "Hi, I'm _______, and I'm an alcoholic/addict." I remember saying, "My name is Chelsey, and I like crack." There were lots of laughs and smiles. I smirked, but it wasn't funny. It was true, and it was shameful. There was no way in hell I was letting any of these people close to my emotions.

I was reintroduced to twelve-step meetings, which were held in abundance in the small Arizona town. It was deemed the "recovery capital" of the United States back in 2010, and it was easy to see why. At every coffee shop in town there were twelve-step members working from *The Big Book of Alcoholics Anonymous*, groups of treatment centers serving food at the soup kitchen, and young people everywhere who were seemingly recovering from addiction. This tight-knit community really held me up when I was certain there was no other way to live other than active addiction and abuse.

The first few weeks were difficult to adjust to; the obsessive need to speak to my abuser was uncontrollable. I would sneak around the house, ensuring that the "house mom" was back in her private suite. I grabbed the white cordless phone and slipped into my hiding spot, the pantry. My hands shook as I dialed his number. Sometimes he would answer and other times not. Several times he accused me of leaving him in a helpless state; other times his mouth was loaded with powerful, verbal assault. Regardless of which way the calls went, I would hyperventilate afterward and harshly ask what was wrong with me. I would get in trouble each time I was caught; not one staff member sought to understand the emotional depth of the pain I was in.

The longer I remained in treatment, the more "freedoms" I was granted. After the first couple months, I was "allowed" to go to outside twelve-step meetings in the community. Several of us were sitting around a campfire meeting where a young woman spoke about her sobriety and her milestone of one year sober. A rush of doubt went through my body. *She must be lying. If she drank and used drugs the way I did, there was no way she hasn't taken at least one sip in a year.*

But she continued to speak about the chaos, abuse, and self-hatred while she was in active addiction, about how she blacked out and woke up with no knowledge of what took place for hours and sometimes days. She described coming to and realizing the harm she had caused to herself and others, but with no ability to stop the self-destruction. I stared at her with tears overflowing my lower lids; I had experienced everything she was talking about. She was the first person I ever heard articulate it out loud. As she shared her past behaviors and degree of instability, I had small moments of realization that other people suffered in similar ways as I had—especially as it related to her desire to black out when she drank. I'd originally started to drink all those years ago so that I could feel free, careless, and fun, but as time went on, the only thing I sought from alcohol was complete black-out. I'd reached the point in my drinking that if I only had time or availability for one drink, I would turn it down. What was the point? The anxiety that would course through my body if I was not able to drink or use as much as I wanted was unbearable.

She was the first woman who ever stated this exact thing when sharing her experience with alcohol and drugs. Her name was Kelsey, and she and I clicked quickly. She was so bubbly, friendly, and open—the opposite of what I felt at that time. She started dragging me everywhere that young people in recovery went: coffee shops, yoga, bowling, speaker meetings, game nights, dances, hikes, and more meetings. I went with her almost everywhere for the first six months of my sobriety. I followed her blindly because something about her made me feel okay. She was relentless in making me feel like I belonged. And while I remained suspicious of joy and skeptical of connection, I still found myself struggling to be comfortable in my own skin. Looking back, I really do attribute the small shifts in my comfortability around others to her.

Despite being surrounded by people, I still found myself struggling to be comfortable in my own skin. While I deeply missed my friends back home, I started to accept that maybe home was not the best place for me to live. Despite my sobriety, I was flooded daily with terrible memories of home. I had a sinking feeling that the familiar bars and party houses, the toxic people, and my ex held too strong of a hold over me that I would never be able stay sober there. As cliché as it sounds, in Arizona, I was separated by a border where he could not cross but back home, we were separated by only my self-will.

During one of the daily group therapy sessions I attended, we were all given a piece of paper with a checklist of types of traumas that we had endured. I checked off every single example that was listed on the sheet. I recall mindlessly marking the sheet and handing it back to the group facilitator. After a glance, he stated, "I don't think I have had anyone mark off everything." While his statement struck me as odd, I remained emotionless. Uncertain what the exact purpose of the assignment was, I folded that piece of paper when he handed it back to me and put it in my purse, feeling that at some point, I would need that reminder.

THE WEIGHT OF EXPECTATIONS

At the end of my time in treatment, I had achieved six months of continuous sobriety. I was in disbelief that I had gone that long without a drink or a drug. Like a good student, I jumped in with both feet into my AA program. I worked diligently with my sponsor and even sponsored several other women in the community. I attended meetings daily, held service commitments, and prayed multiple times a day to a God I did not believe in. I'd grown up with very minimal exposure to religion or discussion of God, so praying felt like a foreign process, one that made me deeply uncomfortable.

Day after day, I felt minimal "relief" from prayer and reliance on a higher power as it related to my mental and emotional health. My sponsors and other members of the twelve-step community reminded me repeatedly that the further away I got from "God," the closer I was to a drink. This sentiment kept me fearful enough to continue praying to something I did not believe in.

Despite my action-oriented perfectionism, my intuition was always nudging at me; there was more to my recovery than AA. The emotional freedom that other people in twelve-step programs discussed was only felt by half of me while the other half was stuck, waiting for the next shoe to drop. I was perpetually stuck in a heightened state of alertness, on guard, consumed with a sense of impending danger. I was stricken with flashbacks and deeply terrified of what my body felt.

This internal conflict defined the next several years of my recovery. I lived like a ping pong ball, bouncing between confusing thoughts, feelings, and memories with little conviction that the solution or treatment for me was in the twelve steps. I knew for many years using drugs and alcohol were a necessity for me; they helped decrease the emotional pain that haunted me and allowed me to separate from the traumas I had experienced. What I was not clear on was what came first: life's afflictions or the desire to drink.

Very few people around me discussed their traumatic pasts or the impact that chronic stress and unhealed mental health issues had on their obsessive need for substances. Most of the members of AA were certain that they were all born with alcoholism and would die with the disease, sober or not. Based on the opinions of those around me and the absolute need for me to get sober, it was undeniable at the time that my primary issue was staying sober. Despite an inner knowledge that AA could and would not fully help me heal, I stuck to it with dedication for years.

Sitting in twelve-step meetings became harder for me as the time passed. I was restless, unhappy, and often resentful because I felt utterly misaligned with aspects of the teachings. However, I never wanted to forget that my life once depended on the twelve-step program and its members. The initial connections that I had made allowed me to start the process of trusting others, with men and women from all walks of life. No one's financial or social status mattered. We all united through stories, experiences, laughter, and a desire to live a different life.

TEMPTATION

For a few months after I completed treatment, I had to go back home to Canada to obtain a student visa to finish my education in Arizona. My experience living back home was filled with a lot of challenges and missteps, but also reconnection with family and friends. As soon as I arrived back in my home city, my nervous system reverted to perpetual hypervigilance. A high level of anxiety and fear clouded over me daily, especially with the risk of running into him, which happened twice. The first time, his eyes met mine through the side mirror in the car next to us in the parking lot of the doctor's office. I froze, quite literally, and lost my ability to speak. I don't remember how I communicated to my mom who was next to us, but as soon as she understood, we drove away speedily. Was this a coincidence? Did he know I would be here? Why was "my higher power" doing this to me?

After this incident, my curiosity took over many times, and I found out what I could about him from social media accounts. I would subtly ask old "using friends" about his status; the result of those inquiries left me sick to my stomach and confused. While the city was small, it was big enough to avoid certain parts of town, but despite this fact, I found myself driving by our old house, the gas station down the street, and other areas we would frequent together. As I put my car in park, surveilling my surroundings at the gas station before getting out of the car, I caught his black eyes staring back at me from the car beside me. How was this happening again? My stomach hollowed out and again, I froze. But this time it was not for as long. I was able to recognize him as a danger I should run from, and I pulled out of the parking lot immediately and drove away, looking in my rearview mirror to ensure he wasn't following me.

My perspective of him rapidly grew conflicted after these brief run ins. I had parts of me convincing other parts that there was no danger, that my reasons for feeling terrified were unwarranted. In response, I would be haunted by flashbacks of the horror he exposed me to and the abusive things he did to me. Most days, I was at the mercy of a song on the radio, a flashback I experienced that day, or a thought about someone or something from my time with him.

I was starting to truly understand how contradictory my desires and actions were. I would experience involuntary and unexpected bodily responses or debilitating emotions or memories. The attachment pull felt like heated adrenaline— a deep need to be breathing the same air as him or sensing his energy regardless of its degree of threat. Other times, the shame that flooded me emptied out my core, forcing me to separate from the sexual abuse memories that would overtake me. These experiences often took place shortly after I engaged with his family and friends or inquired about his whereabouts. Meanwhile, AA had drilled into my head to be thoroughly honest about *everything*; if I wasn't, I would surely relapse. But being fully transparent was too risky because no one seemed to understand my words or actions, not even me.

The parts of me that held the traumatic memories had no idea how to be forthright with others because I did not know what the truth was. I would often waver between "that never happened" and "that never happened to me" or "it happened to me but doesn't bother me anymore." I tried talking about it, writing about it, practicing "letting go" exercises, pretending he didn't exist, moving on in a new relationship, and even going to therapy; nothing relieved me of the PTSD symptoms related to our relationship.

At the direction of others in twelve-step programs, I had shared some of my deepest, darkest, and most shameful experiences with women in AA and experienced zero of the relief that was promised, only more terror and shame. Some of the other women had shared pieces of their traumatic events, but most appeared unbothered. This had led to many questions like "Are they lying about what they shared?", "Am I weaker than them?", or "Why aren't I experiencing the relief they appear to have?"

SHAME

Prior to me leaving for back home, I had met someone. We had met outside an AA meeting through mutual friends. His face was drawn, pale, and respectfully standoffish. He had just experienced a relapse on heroin and was coming back to active recovery. Despite his demeanor, something inside of me was interested in getting to know him more—and I quickly learned that the feeling was mutual. Kyle and I hit it off immediately.

When I first arrived back in Arizona to finish school, I was eager to solidify my worth through sleeping with Kyle. We had been talking through Skype the entire time I was in Canada, building an authentic friendship and the beginning of a romantic relationship. When he said no and suggested we wait to sleep with one another, I was flabbergasted and ridden with shame, shutting down completely.

While he knew some of my history and was being respectful to me, he also valued intimacy in a way that I couldn't.

I laid on the bed of his small apartment, rapidly looking around the room for an exit. In that moment, what felt like a hundred thoughts swirled around in my mind. I didn't even enjoy sex or want to be intimate with anyone, yet it was what I knew as the "right" thing to do when with a man. I felt betrayed by my own body; I deeply hated the very act of sex and felt revolted by the same act that I felt driven to carry out with Kyle. I desperately wanted to escape myself for days afterward, the rapid fire of flashbacks was overwhelming, yet I didn't know how to share this with anyone. No one around me understood the magnitude of what I felt because it wasn't logical; it was all rooted in the complexities of surviving sexual trauma.

Despite my deep sense of rejection, Kyle and I continued in our relationship. We would talk for hours in his old, beat-up '92 Honda Accord, Blink 182 or similar artists on the tape track and a cigarette lit. We would drive up and down the roads in the hills surrounding Prescott, parking in different spots, watching the stars. He never once pushed me to be intimate, and he demonstrated true respect toward me, which was a brand-new experience for me. The level of safety I was building with him was the blueprint I needed to even begin healing my wounds.

Despite the security I was starting to feel, I would flip and switch and start pushing him away, my body ignited with a compulsive desire to be alone, untouched, and invisible to him. When he reacted with caring and calm energy, attempting to understand me, I would respond with even more intensity. A part of me would watch him, his face etched with pain and confusion as I spit horrid things at him. My heart ached but I couldn't stop what came out of my mouth. These patterns increased my self-hatred, and I would often stumble into the shower, avoiding the mirror and sitting on the bottom of the porcelain tub, scrubbing as hard as I could to rid my skin of the grossness and shame that infiltrated it.

I was utterly confused with myself. I would crave and obsess about the security of our relationship with no evidence that it wasn't secure. Other times, I would threaten to leave the relationship for any reason that didn't feel right, including mundane things such as a messy kitchen. These fast switches in my perspective were truly uncontrollable and led to either complete shutdown, panic attacks, or explosive behavior that was not congruent with the circumstances. There were several times that Kyle would break down with fear, pain, and confusion; he explained it like he was on a rollercoaster ride with no ability to stop it. His inability to make sense of my behaviors, which were alarmingly out of character and disoriented to our reality, was overwhelming. We both lacked true understanding of the nuances of complex trauma and dissociation.

I had two different parts of me with glaringly opposite beliefs about relationships. This realization really hit me hard the day that I "left" due to a messy kitchen. As I walked angrily down the street, he followed in his car, patiently waiting for me to change my mind and get in. The Arizona sun was beating down on me, and I eventually chose to get back in his car to go home. Incidents like these weren't rare, but over time, Kyle and I learned our own way to navigate them while remaining committed to one another.

The betrayal wounds that shaped my perspective of romantic relationships resulted in a lot of displaced rage and blame. I used to think that the shame I felt was a direct result of the anger I spewed onto people, but as I learned more about the nuances of complex trauma and dissociation, I was able to recognize that shame as an emotion was so intolerable to me that rage had to step in for my self-preservation.

My shame came from

being ridiculed and embarrassed.

being exploited.

being sexually used and abused.

being abused in front of others.

losing agency over my body.

And, eventually, shame shaped my reactions to others and life experiences.

When the emotional brick fortress wasn't guarding all aspects of myself, I felt an overwhelming desperation to be seen, understood, and validated by Kyle. Again, he was tossed into a tornado of my changing expectations, leaving him questioning himself and his abilities as my partner. I would animatedly deny any wrongdoing on my part when these personality switches would happen, mostly because I did not remember when I was in the other perspective. I felt confused daily, about my own thoughts, reactions, emotional state, and why others had certain opinions about who I was.

It became second nature to "front" and pretend that I was okay and bypass the lack of memory I had. I experienced frequent blackout periods of not only memory but the emotions associated with them. This ability to either numb or completely shove away hard memories and feelings was useful when separating from a painful experience or memory allowing the felt senses to fade just as hastily as they came in. But when attempting to build new relationships and maintain other ones, this ability brought a lot of challenges.

There were several times when I would become aware of different distinct perspectives I held; these moments would flood my entire sense of being with a sense of emptiness. It felt like all I could do was beg my brain and body to stop responding in unpleasant and terrifying ways. It happened often enough that it became my coping skill—sharing the stress load between various parts of my mind's way of continuing.

I felt aware of several versions of myself at once, all trying to share one body and mind, fighting to be first in line, to be heard and understood. When the overwhelming feeling of being a jigsaw puzzle that was missing pieces took over, my bed became my best friend. I would crawl under the covers, hold my hands over my ears, and desperately plead for the internal noise to stop. I quickly realized that being stuck in a state of immobility was not conducive with the level of functioning I desired, and this led me to aligning with the one part of me who could pretend, who could mask, and (most importantly) who could be productive, interactive, and seemingly put together.

WHEN IT'S TOO MUCH

Facebook memories can be my worst nightmare. They remind me of events that I have no explicit memory of. When I first got sober, I assumed that most of my amnesia was related to substance abuse and would often laugh at the things that would pop up on my Facebook account. Sometimes I would be embarrassed, regretful, and even shocked at the events I participated in and the people I surrounded myself with. However, when I started to notice moments of amnesia in sobriety, I felt frightened and confused.

Equating amnesia to trauma was not in the forefront of my mind, nor was it ever discussed with any therapist I had seen. I could list a series of events that I "knew" I attended, experiences I had (such as my own wedding and certain vacations) but I could not "feel" the memory; I was confused why I couldn't even remember positive things in my life. While I would hear my husband, friends, and family recount the actual lived experiences of life, I pretended that I related. This caused me to create narratives along the way. I wasn't trying to lie; I was attempting to piece together experiences so I could feel a sense of "knowing."

There are many events, positive and negative, that would have never crossed my mind again unless I had been reminded of them. I realized that I could easily remember faces but had no recollection of my interactions with them or how I knew them. When I came across different people who I must have met at some point, they could pick up where we left off, but I had to scramble to put the pieces together so I didn't appear completely void of reality. Worst of all was my inability to keep a calendar. I was constantly forgetting and then secretly rearranging plans so these faults were not discovered. I hated being seen in a light that was less than perfect.

There were entire events that I had no memory of *experiencing*, such as concerts, weddings, bachelorette parties, trips, and more. I could get away with covering my symptoms up by having enough of the information of what happened or jumping into a story being told my someone else and casually adding something that "might" fit.

I consistently felt pulled to meet the expectations outlined by AA and being honest with myself about what I needed to feel emotional freedom from my own pain. Reclaiming my pain as mine was a challenge that took many years. The dissociative processes that I had developed were the power force of my brain.

Separating myself from the overwhelming pain of traumatic experiences became my forte; it felt essential for survival and any sort of present-day functioning. Learning to gain back the personal agency that my abusers had taken from me was a terrifying road to recovery. Saying no, arguing, attempting to leave, or even crying for him to stop had done nothing to stop his actions and had often made things worse. I'd learned to drift off into another world during the abuse or experienced a sense of leaving my body. Alcohol and drugs had helped too.

Over time, I'd learned different strategies and tactics to try and make his unpredictable behavior more predictable; sometimes they'd worked and other times it hadn't. Unfortunately, I wasn't new to the notion that certain men thrived off control and ego centric behavior. I was eventually able to use this to my advantage to step around the land mines at times. This "part" or "aspect" of my personality became fully developed at some point throughout my relationship with him; it held many of the memories, actions, and behaviors because of the chronic sexual abuse.

As I continued in my recovery journey, I was flooded daily with overwhelming somatic and emotional symptoms but with little ability to articulate why; my voice had been stolen. I would see my abuser in my dreams and wake up shaking, heavy breathing flooded with terror, convincing myself that if I looked over, he would be there instead of Kyle. During a difficult several months, I even started to hallucinate him in our room. His head would be floating in the corner by the door, leaving me too paralyzed to get out of bed. By the time I had the courage to wake Kyle up, the image faded. And there I was again, convinced that I was going crazy or developing schizophrenia. How could this be happening when I had achieved over three years sober?

It felt like parts of my mind continued to deny that what had happened was traumatic at all, but other parts kept showing me the realities of what took place. I always felt confused about what was real and what wasn't, both in the past and present. In the beginning of my relationship with Kyle, I displayed a lot of startling behavior. I cannot begin to count the number of times that I threatened to break up with him, ran away from our apartment convinced that he did something wrong or hurled verbal nastiness at him in hopes of him leaving me. Being approached by Kyle for a hug, a gentle kiss, or any sort of intimacy sent me right back into defense mode or a state of complete dissociation, disconnecting from any sense of self.

My internal experiences weren't much different from what I displayed outwardly. Chaos filled my mind, but thankfully, many days I was able to lock it away securely in a box. When some trigger or event opened the box, the overwhelming need to crawl out of my own skin took over. Eventually, I would switch into a state that was void of emotions and connection to anything painful, moving through the day like nothing was wrong. To most people, these shifts were very subtle and typically went unnoticed, but Kyle almost always knew. He felt helpless, not knowing how he could help because we both lacked a true understanding of what was happening.

I continued to dissociate from any intimate experience, coming out of it crying, shaking, and scared. These events were perplexing because I was not in danger with Kyle. I wanted to be intimate with him, I knew that I was safe, but my body told me another story. To make things more complicated, a part of me craved control and abuse from Kyle because it was predictable and familiar, but there was not an abusive bone in his body. Those close to me in my recovery circle had no idea how to respond to me when I would discuss these impulses. Additionally, it seemed that every therapist could only take my healing so far and was stuck in how to guide me outside of suggesting that I avoid sexual intimacy for the time being, passively suggesting that these symptoms would go away at some point.

Kyle and I trudged in that space for a long time, consistently looking for balance between what was tolerable for me and what was needed for a relationship. While Kyle never once demanded anything from me, he verbalized how important it was for him to connect with me. Hearing intimacy and connection in the same sentence sent my nervous system into a different realm and enraged me because, in my mind, those two things did not go together.

I'M STILL HERE

Authentically connecting with newer people in my life (who hadn't been with me since the beginning of time) was tremendously challenging for me. I knew deep down that my best friends from back home would walk to the end of the earth with me, but that type of loyalty felt impossible to build with others. They didn't know my heart, my true self, who I was before the traumas. Most people interpreted my personality as unapproachable, cold, and sometimes harsh. It pained me to be seen this way because I desperately wanted people to realize that I wasn't choosing to be stuck in this state and often felt like there was no way out.

New friends even warned me that if I didn't change my behavior, I would lose my relationship with Kyle. Losing him was truly the last thing I wanted, but I struggled so badly to change my irrational responses and displaced emotions from the past to the present. It took a lot of mental work to remain connected to my surroundings and the present-day relationships that I was supposed to be nurturing.

If I wasn't in a state of hypervigilance and seeing the world through a distrusting lens, I would vacillate between being overly functioning or shut down. In conjunction with my conflicting states of functioning, I would lash out in rage and anger for reasons that were not congruent with events happening around me. If I sensed any sort of dishonesty, confusion or hurt with anyone, I would act out in a way that would put a strong wall in between us. This result was a twofold experience to me; a part of me wanted a permanent barrier between me, and another just wanted to be understood.

I had zero awareness of how deeply dissociated and disoriented I was. My level of amnesia was significant, and I would forget things I was told and told others minutes, hours, and days earlier. Due to the perpetual nature of the sexual trauma I had survived, remaining disconnected from my body was my go-to response. This was partially due to the genital pain I would feel for no known reason, the disgust I felt when seeing myself naked, going to the bathroom, or being in my cycle. To get through these natural and common experiences of the human body, it was necessary for me to completely disconnect from myself. I walked around completely separated from my physical body; I would trip over my own feet, bang my head getting into the car or on the cupboards, and was fully void of spatial awareness.

I write these sentences now with a level of awareness that I did not have for the years while I was stuck in tiresome flashbacks and somatic reliving episodes. Eventually, I learned that most of my personality changes were automatic and unconscious processes. It took me years to accept that I was a victim of repetitive and sadistic domestic violence. I had told many people over the years how awful he was, I could retell fragments of events, but articulating the details and specifically how the trauma impacted me was next to impossible. Sometimes it still is.

I tirelessly searched for a therapist who could help. I asked everyone I knew in AA. The intensity of my symptoms felt unmanageable and often came out in bouts of rage. I was deteriorating mentally but adamantly refused to admit it.

I was completing my twelve steps with a man in recovery who had thirty-plus years sober. It was suggested to me to work with him because my rage was like a "man's," not a typical woman's. As I type this sentence, my skin crawls because the belief that I was not allowed to express intense emotion because that was "untraditional" for a woman felt like another way to shut down what I felt.

I complied for several months with this belief, once again feeling separated and judged by some of the women in AA due to being "different" for having a male sponsor. AA was extremely cliquey at times, reminding me of high school where everyone was quick to judge, believe they knew what was best for everyone, and many had no problems breaking down the faults of others.

No one around me would acknowledge the anger and rage I felt as a symptom of unhealed trauma; I was repeatedly taught to get out of "victim mode" because I would never heal if I didn't. It seemed that no one wanted to ever discuss what happened to them in childhood or throughout active addiction; it was easier for most to connect through telling "war stories" about their chaotic behaviors while actively addicted, ones that made them fit in with the crowd.

This milieu was focused on changing behavior, forgiving, and taking accountability for our actions. Many of these concepts did not feel congruent with what I had been through. Why was I being encouraged to make amends to a man who sexually, physically, and emotionally abused me for years? Theoretically, I was supposed to make amends to anyone I had a resentment toward, including my drug dealers, abusers, and very unhealthy people. Without this vital step, many people told me that I would not stay sober because I hadn't experienced enough humility.

I would spend hours putting pen to paper, writing out my steps, especially my fourth step and attempting to make sense of the "my part" column. Did the AA community not understand what it is like to be physically and mentally trapped while experiencing such horrible abuse? According to them, my part was that I stayed and engaged. This rhetoric played into the painful confusion I felt regarding the unnecessary responsibility I took for experiencing abuse at the hand of others.

When I functioned from a present adult state, I was logical, attentive, enjoyable, and understandable; when I was stuck in a state related to trauma and abuse, I was often unrecognizable or masking the insanity I was feeling within. I started to feel like I could not trust myself. I became scared of what I could say or do and would rather be stuck in a "season" where I had no past at all. There were many days when triggers seemed to be in the past and others where they engulfed my every thought and move.

ONE SPLIT LIFE

Our life in Prescott was simple. We had a host of friends and acquaintances, we both held jobs in recovery centers, I was completing college, and we kept dreaming of what sobriety would continue to gift us. We had very little money, but it didn't matter. There was an element of safety that I was building in my new life, and I was grateful.

Kyle proposed after we had been together for one year, and I immediately said yes. I wish I could say I had no doubts, but I was riddled with them: When was I going to meet the other "side" of the man I was going to marry? Was he going to cheat? Relapse? Leave me? Become bored with me or sick of me?

While I had always wanted to get married and have a family, the scars that I had collected over the years had left me with significant doubts regarding my long-term worth to anyone. To the contrary, the "part" of self that did not have access to any sort of trauma held quite a different perspective, one that was more "traditional" and harsh, including punitive thoughts about our lack of financial security, his age (he was twenty-two at this time while I was twenty-five) and lack of career, the fact we hadn't known one another long, and questions about when would he be ready for kids (with some self-righteousness belief that I already was). All of these mental tactics helped me keep myself protected from some degree of anticipated emotional injury.

The *truth* of how I felt was different from both previously described perspectives; I was elated, I couldn't wait to wedding plan, and I was unbelievably grateful that someone as kind as Kyle wanted to share a life with me.

Navigating these rapid—often conflicting—thoughts was a daily struggle in the life of my fragmented mind. Invisible to the naked eye but all consuming for me, I fought myself many times, screaming at various versions of myself to all agree with one another. It often felt impossible to function in a romantic relationship.

Unfortunately, complicating the internal dialogue more, there were degrees of amnesia between these perspectives, parts of me would entirely forget that I had no access to the other thoughts and feelings. There were times that I would "come to" sobbing or angry with no idea why I was feeling these things. The severe amnesia-based symptoms caused immense confusion not only for me but for Kyle as well. Being married to one person with such glaring sides to their personality was emotionally draining and impacted his self-confidence and worth as my spouse.

Despite these challenges, the core of our relationship was stable, and we loved one another deeply. However, when I would switch emotional states, he had zero clue how to appropriately intervene. He had no professional support or guidance, only from men in AA who mostly misguided him with "advice"—suggesting that I was mean, unfair, and had to change for him to stay in a relationship with me.

While I did need to "change" for our relationship to withstand time, it wasn't a choice that I had full access to regardless of how bad I wanted it. Since my behaviors didn't align with the twelve steps and what they called "God's will," I started to recoil from specific people in AA and created a mask to wear around others.

At the same time, I had become a pillar in the recovery community, sponsoring half of the women in town, attending meetings daily, and holding an abundance of volunteer commitments. Living from a set of principled and disciplined behaviors continued to propel me forward in life and achieve college graduation, job stability, and a thriving life, but it held me back in other aspects of my healing.

At this point in my recovery, I had a difficult time correlating the severe somatic symptoms I suffered from daily to the unhealed stuff I buried deep down. I had become a master answering the question "How are you?" from a cognitive perspective only: the words "I am great!" and "I am good!" would always come out of my mouth. I felt like I was two different people, the person that presented herself to the world and the woman I experienced within; the mismatch was daunting and confusing.

The "split" within myself felt unavoidable. It was impossible to be connected to things from my past and continue forward in my relationships and life. The felt sense of dissociative splitting was uncomfortable and terrifying at times. I would see my husband's loving face in front of me, recognize my level of safety but continue to feel like I needed to rip my own skin off because I was dirty and ashamed. Slivers of memories of traumatic sexual experiences would intrude in a flash and then rapidly recede, taking my breath away and regrettably reminding me of the danger of people. I would stare at my shoes, my hands, the ground, anything to ground myself in the here and now, but unfortunately my orientation to time was not accurate and I would see hands that were years younger, shoes that were stuck in a room with an abuser, and the ground felt like it just didn't exist. Recognizing my body meant that I had to realize what happened to my body at the hands of others, and this was entirely too painful.

Common grounding exercises were not effective for me, which confused those around me who could practice mindfulness, meditation, and breathwork and feel relief. Despite their hopes for me and private assurances, my dissociation symptoms only increased, and I was the furthest thing from "meditated." Some days I figured I was just stubborn and suffered from black-and-white thinking, refusing to participate in activities that could possibly help me. However, as I grew to understand dissociative processes, I learned that meditation could exacerbate existing dissociative symptoms such as derealization and depersonalization.

I had minimal understanding of the concept of self. Others would reflect on how much I seemed to "know" about myself and admired my ability to self-reflect, but they were wrong. Some days, these observations led me to feel like a fraud and a liar because those people didn't know the truth. While I did understand some things about myself cognitively, I had almost zero ability to connect to my emotions as they related to events.

I often spoke about myself like I would a storyline in a book or film. This allowed me to thrive in twelve-step programs. I was a dedicated sponsor and helper and strong advocate for sobriety and healing, but behind closed doors, I still functioned from a place of self-rejection and shame. I don't think anyone around me would guess that I struggled with esteem or confidence; they assumed I solely suffered with a bad attitude, lack of caring, and rage. While I knew these behaviors were often my go-to defense strategies for self-protection, most people around me did not and judged me in hurtful ways.

UNEASE

Some of my most painful and confusing moments throughout my early recovery included being flooded with somatic sensations without a clear-cut narrative—meaning I didn't have a fully developed story to attach to the feeling. Without a narrative, it was "easier" to suppress, ignore, and dismiss because I could repeatedly lie to myself that what I was feeling had to be linked to something else and not PTSD.

I was stuck in a state of hypervigilance toward Kyle and every move he made, the moods he was in, and the tone of voice he spoke with. Rarely would he use a stern or harsh tone; rather, a confused and desperate sadness filled his voice as he watched me become someone different from five minutes prior. The reactions that Kyle would get from me were everchanging and many times unexpected. Objects would go flying from the hidden rage, my body would often brace for impact and hide under my covers with no precipitating reasoning; other times, it was common for me to pull away from any type of intimacy and even hold my fists up to "protect" myself.

Walking from a parked car at night to the front door of any "place" sent me into complete panic. Fear engulfed me even if it wasn't congruent with the then. Darkness, aloneness, and togetherness—all led to inner conflict that left me fighting the voices in my head. I would bang on our apartment door from the inside to scare away any "bad guy" on the other side before every cigarette I smoked. My heart raced and my eyes darted around as I tried to visually map out an escape route any time I entered a new space. These strong somatic symptoms led to my words never coming out right. I could rarely verbalize what I was so petrified of. The whirlwind of thoughts, somatic feelings, and logic all contradicted one another, leading me to shut down in it all.

At the time, I had zero concept of what masking was. However, as my inner world felt uneasy and the very existence in my own body felt scary, I had to present as if I was okay to survive the next moment. People close to me were rarely allowed to see into my troubled mind, only the unwelcome behaviors that they assumed I could control; they saw me as on edge and irritated, reactive, or difficult to have a conversation with. Despite validity in my behaviors being very challenging and distressing, I was often trying to "manage" everything going on inside my mind. Much of it didn't make logical sense. In those moments, I felt extremely misunderstood and judged, but over time, I was rightfully forced to acknowledge that my treatment of others was often unjust and unfair.

There were questions I didn't have language for back then, but they lived in me all the same—loud, confusing, and unresolved.

INNER CONFLICT

Living with inner conflict is like waking up each day unsure of who you are or how you'll feel about something. I could hold deep love and deep fear in the same breath. Parts of me would beg for connection, while others would prepare for abandonment. My reactions felt like they came from different versions of me—each with a voice, a memory, and a need that I couldn't always track.

DISCONNECTION

How can you know something but not feel connected to it? I could say what happened. I could name the trauma, tell the story. But it didn't land in my body like truth. It was like I had read about it in someone else's diary—close enough to see, far enough to stay numb. I'd speak the words but feel blank inside.

NO CONTROL OVER RAGE EPISODES

I didn't feel like I was choosing anger. It would come in waves—sudden, hot, and terrifying. I'd be screaming before I knew what set me off and then dissociating just as fast. Sometimes I didn't even remember the full episode. I hated how unpredictable I felt and how much shame followed.

CONSTANT CONFUSION

When you are caught in a cycle of dissociation, there's no stable center to return to. I was always asking: Is this real? Did that happen? Who was I then, and who am I now? Trying to explain dissociation to others felt impossible because it barely made sense to me.

DOUBTING MY REALITY

Some memories came like snapshots: standing at a door, hiding in a closet, someone yelling. Others came with sensations: tight chests, held breath, a smell I couldn't place. But none of it felt complete, and all of it felt questionable. I doubted myself constantly.

LIVING WITH DISSOCIATION

Dissociation is not just "zoning out." It's being disconnected from your body, your feelings, even your voice. I could be mid conversation and suddenly feel like I wasn't there anymore. I was present but gone. Functioning but unreachable. Other times, I would tap into a part of me whose job was to be superwoman—achieving everything I possibly could in a day, without blinking an eye or feeling an emotion.

LITTLE MEMORY OF CHILDHOOD

My childhood doesn't play like a movie. It's a series of fragments, scattered with brief warmth and then anxiety. I can recall several good moments, but they're layered with unease.

NOT RECOGNIZING MYSELF

Sometimes I didn't know who I was. I'd look in the mirror and feel like I was seeing someone else. I'd read things I wrote and have no memory of writing them. I would be told about conversations I had but have no connection to them. The past didn't feel like mine, and the present didn't always make sense.

MASKING MY AMNESIA

I found myself seeing people who looked familiar but were unplaceable by me. Unfortunately, they often recognized me. They could remember what we talked about—short stories I shared about my family, friends, and career—but I could not remember anything but a flash of their face. My stomach would start to sink and remind me of the degree of my amnesia; something was wrong with the way I processed my days. I started to feel extremely embarrassed in these moments because I was certain that people could tell and my masking abilities were crumbling.

As an adult, I made up narratives (based in reality) due to the long periods of time with missing memory, both long term and short term. Sometimes it was answering the question "How was your weekend?" with a simple reply of "Good!" with zero recollection of what occurred. Other times it was telling everyone from the AA podium that my childhood was perfect, and my problem was solely the fact that I liked drugs and alcohol. This was a fascinating approach to my addiction and mental health journey, complete emotional amnesia from my own traumatic experiences that influenced my maladaptive coping skills. There was always a small voice, a splinter of realization that told me this wasn't true, but I couldn't access anything explicit about the "truth," so I paved my own as I went.

Intimacy was the area where my somatic symptoms wreaked the most havoc on my life. Throughout my abusive relationships, I only engaged because the consequences of not engaging would be too difficult to endure. My nervous system was always on high alert for every move Kyle made; it had been trained that way. If I looked over and saw Kyle's hands moving toward me, I assumed I had a role to play. Despite the inaccuracy of this, I would treat him like such. A perceived facial expression—such as indifference or, worse, unhappiness—sent parts of me into a complete tailspin. Panic ensued if I sensed even a bit of melancholy due to the consequences of what my body anticipated would happen next. Despite the realism of these fears and somatic senses, the reality was that I was never in danger with Kyle and never would be. Some days it felt like I was speaking different languages within my own self; parts of me could not agree on anything regarding romance, intimacy, or love.

STABLE ENOUGH

Despite my emotional chaos, the relationship blueprint with Kyle was strong, predictable, and safe. We both got our first jobs in the recovery field at the same substance use treatment center, and I was enrolled back in college to finish the last year of my undergraduate degree in psychology. Despite being grossly underpaid and undertrained in the position I held, I started to feel effective and confident in my ability to attune to others who were struggling.

I was thrown into the work with zero training and only basic support and supervision. Despite these downfalls, the clients taught me a lot about a career in psychotherapy. The continued relapses, the emotional despair, PTSD symptoms, mental health conditions that required medication, and more were not being effectively treated by sitting in a room full of other drugs addicts and alcoholics. I started to build a deeper understanding of the degree of emotional pain people suffered from due to unhealed trauma, complex family dynamics, and addictive behaviors. It turns out that the people's pain I related to the most were my own clients; the unhealed baggage I was dragging around was constantly reflected in their stories. I had moments of wishing that it was acceptable for me to act out in the self-destructive ways I witnessed them using; I still desperately wanted relief from myself.

Despite my own emotional turmoil, this season of time in our life granted me a level of humility that I needed to develop independence and drive to continue growing. Kyle and I went without a lot of tangible items that we wanted: we managed our small salaries with an envelope system, lived in a run-down apartment unit, and shared a car that was old and stained with the smell of cigarettes. Our date nights included dinner at Denny's, or if we felt like splurging, we went to Red Lobster. Despite a lack of financial security, we had an abundance of other important things. I was taught that gratitude was a touchstone of living a more fulfilled and stable life. I rode this wave for many years.

Friends and acquaintances came and went in Prescott, mainly due to relapse or death by overdose. Almost every week in a twelve-step meeting, someone would share that they lost a friend, roommate, or family member to a drug overdose. The emotional toll of such frequent losses kicked me back into a state of numbness. This wasn't abnormal. I watched my close friends and the recovery community do the same thing, barricade difficult emotions out and focus solely on actions they could take to remain sober and not be a "statistic."

Most of the women who surrounded me were traumatized and disconnected from themselves, they just didn't know it. We were all in long-term relationships or marriages and had an appearance of stable, healed, and forthcoming about our authentic selves. As the years passed and personal defects became more apparent, I started to feel that I did not know many of the people I surrounded myself with. Friends started to relapse and attempt to drink normally; these notions really shook up my sense of hope for long-term sobriety. I was witness to alarming behavior from those I thought I knew, the division of "perfect" marriages, and the secrets and lies of many; I began to think that maybe there was a lot more to what was "wrong with us" than just substance use.

I originally sought treatment because I was quite literally dying. As I watched the emotional struggles of those around me, my curiosity grew about how they felt on the inside. I went through periods of talking about trauma as a general topic more openly, but when those around me said very little about their histories besides the amount of drugs they used or the impact of their past, I felt alone and learned to close my mouth. I was confused why and how others seemed to have full control of their behaviors while I didn't.

BREATHING AND BREAKING AWAY

After I graduated, we began to have dreams outside of small-town life. Kyle and I discussed moving somewhere else to branch away from what felt like broken friendships and limitations living where we were. We dreamed big with slight delusion on the easiness of our dream; we were going to open our own substance abuse treatment center in another state and provide true "co-occurring" treatment. We attempted to find funding from multiple different sources. We had secured and lost two investments over a few weeks; one was days prior to our move date. There was a small voice in my head that said, "I told you so" and "This isn't possible."

Family and friends questioned what seemed like a "sudden" decision to make, one that took us away from the stability and safety in the sober community of our small town. From the first few months in recovery up until the day we moved, the AA community explicitly taught that staying sober without the harsh accountability of the people who "knew us best" was virtually impossible.

We struggled to break free from this messaging for a long time after we moved. I was full of culpability regarding my choice to leave the women in AA and close friends. Kyle struggled to find his footing with new people in a different recovery community. While I found a new "AA community," I consistently found myself judging the suggestions of twelve-step programs and feeling misaligned. Most of my emotional struggles had little to do with a drink or a drug but rather emotional health around interpersonal relationships and toward myself.

Living in Colorado was a growing experience for us as individuals and as a couple. Breathing the mountain air reminded me of home in Canada, the restaurant scene in Denver was incredible, and a few of our close friends moved there around the same time to open treatment centers too. It was 2015 and, unfortunately, opening substance use treatment centers was an epidemic. Insurance fraud was happening all around the country with insurance plans paying astronomical prices to treatment providers who were not held accountable for the quality of services being provided. Each treatment program was run by "recovering addicts" with no college degree in business or psychology/counseling. Thousands of young kids died due to the fraudulent practice of both privately and state-owned treatment centers. The act of client brokering was rampant, some would encourage their potential client to get high and come back in the next day so the treatment center could bill at a higher insurance rate, others paid for a client to get insurance so that the treatment would be reimbursed at a rate of the center's choice; people's lives had, yet again, become a business in America.

There were a handful of us who sought to change that and provide clinical services by licensed professionals and not just by individuals who have a degree in the lived experience of addiction. After a few bumps in the road, our dream took off. We worked hard, putting in way too many hours of work a week with little if any time for self-care. I was completing my Master of Social Work program at this time at Case Western Reserve University via their well-known virtual program, including a practicum at a domestic violence shelter in downtown Denver.

The domestic violence shelter was a large Victorian house. Despite the beauty, the property felt ominous; it creaked, shook, and produced noises that weren't normal. There were many old and current stories of residents seeing ghosts of past women and children who were murdered by their abusers or had died in other ways. Most evenings there was only one of us on staff. I would vigilantly watch the cameras, ensuring no repeat vehicles were circling the property and that there weren't men on foot looking over the fences.

Many of the women engaged in whatever type of work they could to earn money to save for a place for them and their children. Unfortunately, this work often put them in a different type of danger, and many wouldn't come back. Sharing space with these women and children who were escaping horror was not easy on my nervous system. The paranoia I used to experience while being outside at night alone returned. My shifts would end around 11 p.m., and leaving the property felt scarier than staying in it. I ensured that Kyle was awake to remain on the phone with me as I ran from the secured property to my car, which was only blocked off by a fence that anyone could jump. I experienced returning flashbacks because of the hypervigilant state I would often stay stuck in long after my shift.

Those around me suggested I was burnt out, would question my ability to manage all we had going on, but I refused to admit that I couldn't handle it all. Dissociation became my main mode of functioning with very little tolerance for anything that would shift me into the reality of present-day stress.

DIPPING MY TOES IN

After a couple years of consistent trauma-based talk therapy in Prescott and one disastrous session of EMDR (Eye Movement Desensitization and Reprocessing), someone suggested that I explore Somatic Experiencing (SE). Flashing back to late 2010, when I was back in Canada for those three months, someone suggested EMDR to me, with good intention. During EMDR, the therapist helps the client recall aspects of a traumatic memory while they enable bilateral (left to right) stimulation using either hand motions, a light bar, or handheld "buzzies." I had a base understanding of the modality, but at only a few months sober, I had not gained an understanding of my dissociation—which severely interrupts the "basic" purpose of EMDR. As soon as the therapist started the "reprocessing," I left my body and became inundated with rapid flashbacks of numerous sexual abuse scenarios; had no choice but to shut down everything. The therapist appeared startled at my response; it was clear that the goal of decreased emotional stress would not be met that day. I don't recall speaking to the therapist in detail about what happened. A part of me remembers trying to disregard my experience as no big deal because I did not want her to feel bad; it was simply not her fault for following basic protocol.

I never went back.

It was 2012 when I entered the Somatic Experiencing providers office. I was greeted by her therapy dog, a goldendoodle, and he brought me immediate relief and comfort. As the therapist entered the room, she instructed him to go lie on his dog bed. I desperately wanted him close to me; he was a protective shield between me and the therapist. I reluctantly provided some of my history with her. I had become skilled at sharing a somewhat linear timeline of events, meaning, I could state approximate years and months that events took place, but that was about it.

Somatic experiencing is a body-oriented approach to healing trauma and chronic stress. The modality works with how trauma is stored in the nervous system and body rather than focusing on details of the "story" of what happened to the client. It is designed to slowly release the survival energy that had become stuck after traumatic events.

I recalled a seamless childhood, no reported sexual abuse, molestation, bullying, accidents, or significant events until my teen years—a complete disconnect from most of what I wrote earlier in this book. I "knew" I had been in a "bad" relationship prior to getting sober but was not truly connected to the impact his torturous actions had on me. The inappropriateness of my relationship in high school, the things I experienced at the hands of high schoolers as a young teenager, or the much older men we partied with had yet to be addressed in therapy, so for years, I continued to think those experiences were "no big deal" and normal. Every professional I had seen thus far seemed to lack the ability to properly and safely explore how being around chronic violence and sick sexual occurrences impacted someone's mind and body.

As we started our first session, the therapist cautioned me that we would take things "slow" and that it wasn't likely for SE work to impact me the way that EMDR had done a year or so prior. I was cautiously optimistic, trusting her professional input. She instructed me to put my palms on my knees and gently rub them. This simple connection to my body sent my nervous system into out-of-control activation; I became so hot that I thought someone was lighting me on fire. A disoriented thought erupted my entire state: "I have knees?" and "There is connection between my torso and legs?"

Horrific flashbacks flooded my mind, and I started to float away from the version of me that was sitting in the chair; I was completely disconnected from my surroundings and myself. The next thing I knew, the therapist was sternly but gently repeating my name over and over. For a split second, I questioned, "Who is Chelsey?" and "Why am I stuck on the ceiling?"

An intense flood of energy went through my body, and I quickly became aware of the therapy dog, the therapist's facial expression of worry, the window looking out into the parking lot, and a few pillows and pieces of décor in her office. At the time, I had no clue what took place, and I'm not sure if the therapist understood the severity of this dissociative experience. I slowly sipped on the bottle of water she handed to me, my heart rate started to slow down, and my breathing regulated enough. After this session, my willingness to engage in somatic work came to a screeching halt. The therapist and I talked a few days later, and she said she had consulted with some colleagues on how to slow down the process for me even more.

After that first terrible session, somehow my body went into autopilot, and I was able to operate my car, find my way home, and make it into my bed, where I curled under the covers. To my apprehension, Kyle sat on the edge of the bed. I desperately wanted him nearby while another aspect of me needed to push him away. I peeked out from under the covers at different points, scanning the room to ensure it was just him in there. He often reassured me by placing his hand on my back with no expectations to engage in discussion. After an hour or two, I slowly started to orient back to my environment and recognize that it was safe to emerge.

The overwhelm wreaked havoc on my body that day and for many therapy sessions afterward, leading to significant impacts on my blood sugar, nervous system dysregulation, and constant level of exhaustion. I continued to attend for a few months, working to build tolerance to process more trauma material. After I felt stable "enough," I decided I did not need therapy anymore and stopped going. It felt like there was an automatic internal threshold of what I was able or allowed to feel again. In addition, I would randomly touch base with my therapist from substance use treatment because he had proven to be "safe enough" and provided adequate feedback to me without diving into more detail. I was still mainly treating my addiction and trauma from a "top down" approach, highly cognitive and behavioral based. While I had gained enough information about the nervous system to understand many of my "responses" to life, the dissociative symptoms I suffered from were never addressed.

When I was first introduced to the workings of my nervous system, the depth of what I was taught was limited to fight, flight, and freeze. I understood this basic ideology, but it left me feeling misunderstood by professionals and the newest "hot approach" to treating trauma. Internally, I felt so much more than fight, flight, freeze, often experiencing too many nervous system changes in quick succession of one another, resulting in an explosion of overpowering feelings and thoughts.

When I would attempt to explore the unstoppable pull toward the abusive relationships, the feedback I would receive from therapists felt misaligned. They often responded with describing fight, flight, and freeze, completely missing what I was trying to express: that I needed to be close to the abuser or else it felt like I would die.

Historically, it felt like there was an internal miswiring that kept me engaged in relationships way past what was best for me. For years, I desired to be wanted by a man but lacked the self-esteem and maturity to reciprocate a "healthy enough" intimate relationship, so I ended up in many "relationships" where my choice was taken from me. I was often scooped up by men who needed someone to control and take advantage of.

I battled an internal war in my head. A part of me desired these cyclical patterns because I had developed familiarity with the chaos, and other parts desired to freeze, avoid, and defend. I also only felt capable of expressing any wants or needs when intoxicated, and typically, in a frantic and desolate manner.

During the early months of recovery, I was termed a "co-sex addict," a "codependent," a "love addict," and (to make it even more confusing) a "love avoidant." When I first entered treatment, I was so desperate to understand myself that I took on too many "titles" to appease the opinions of many professionals. While much of the information they provided could be applied to my thoughts and behaviors, my personal emotional connection to it all was missing.

Additionally, there was always an underlying assumption that I had full control over what was wrong and that it would all be cured by staying sober. Because of this undeveloped link between trauma and addiction, I remained stuck in a mindset that prided people on making the "right" choices. Fast forward to my marriage with Kyle, the internal dance that I felt with him often mimicked what I somatically felt in my abusive relationships, with one major difference: Kyle was not abusive in any way. My body was reenacting a pattern from the past that was not oriented to the present. Everyone around me was confused about my reactions, thought processes, and perception of events. Some days I held onto my convictions so tight, and others, I felt confused and sad.

When we moved to Colorado, I was hyper focused on work and completing my graduate degree. Personal therapy was not on my radar at all. I started attending AA soon after our move and utilized a sponsor for most of my emotional needs. Again, I started to experience a relationship with a sponsor to be an isolating experience. Almost all my present-day struggles had to do with unhealed trauma and not alcoholism. I never questioned my ability to drink normally;

however, I consistently felt misunderstood by those in AA. They also had minimal advice on how to properly guide me. I did not want to leave AA because I was terrified that if I did, I would drink, and I had no place for alcohol in my life. I enjoyed the community that AA brought into our lives, our closest friends were sober, and at that time, I still believed that AA was the most important aspect of my life.

When I first got sober, I was taught that my own thoughts, ideas, and beliefs led to me drinking and using and that I was better off letting others guide my life. Sometimes all I heard was I had to be "controlled" and "told what to do" by others, which was exactly how I had been living for years prior except with an abusive partner. I could accept that I needed guidance on how to stay away from alcohol and drugs, but my mental health struggles and trauma history were consequently at the wayside; abruptly dragging me under when I least expected it.

Despite the extreme lows at times, I would move through them without a major hitch and continue daily living. Most times, I would have slight recollection at best of what I was feeling before an emotional episode of uncontrollable sadness, fear, anxiety, or rage. The person most impacted was always Kyle because he was with me the most and, regrettably, was on the receiving end of many misdirected thoughts and feelings. The level of forgetfulness and amnesia that I was still experiencing with years sober was something I tried to cover up in any attainable way. I had zero idea how to justify to others my lack of memory without triggering significant concern from them. Frankly, I was so sick of struggling at this point in my recovery that it felt safer to just keep my challenges to myself, allowing a handful of people in when it was necessary. And still, only some was shared; Kyle barely knew about the intensity of my internal struggles.

Several months after getting settled in Colorado, I reluctantly found an EMDR therapist who claimed to specialize in medical trauma and was also type 1 diabetic. On the surface, this seemed like a logical match. I assumed since so many years had passed since my first EMDR session that my experience would be different. As soon as the bilateral buzzing of the paddles started, I felt a surge of energy move through my core, then almost immediately, my dissociation kicked in and I felt a version of myself separate from the body sitting in the chair. I was able to observe myself participating in EMDR and communicate to the therapist what was "coming up," even though most of it was what I thought she wanted to hear.

While I certainly wasn't lying about trauma material, I felt a strong sense that she would have no idea how to handle the truth of what I was experiencing, so I faked being more "in touch with myself" than I was. I thanked her for the session and quickly left the office, never returning. Despite my internal world being tumultuous at times, it was recognizable and far more comforting than the unfamiliar world of deep healing. I took a long break from therapy after that session. My trust for clinical professionals was in the toilet, especially after how easy it was for me to derail the session without any seeming sense of my true emotional state.

PART FOUR

family

MORE THAN JUST ME

As Kyle and I began to stabilize financially and see our hard work pay off, we decided that it was time to start planning for kids. Due to an overrun school and work schedule, the trauma symptoms seemed to get tucked away for the next little while, at least from the forefront of my brain. I still suffered from explosive emotions that were not oriented to my current life, but I was completely disconnected from the reality of them being trauma related.

At this time, my diabetes was nowhere near where it needed to be for pregnancy, so that was what we became hyper focused on. I was in such distress at my inability to regulate my blood sugars, I considered finding a treatment center for those who suffer from similar symptoms as me. At the time, I was terrified to take more insulin because more insulin meant weight gain and weight gain was the worst thing to happen to me; it signified complete loss of control over my body. As I did my research, I found many other women who suffered like I did. There was a term for it: diabulimia. The disorder was defined by restricting or limiting insulin intake to lose or manage weight. The conflicting desire to be healthy enough for pregnancy was almost enough for me to change my patterns with insulin and food intake—but not quite. Despite not finding a treatment center that specialized in this condition, I did find a diabetic "bootcamp" at one of the main research hospitals for type 1 diabetes. I decided that this was something I could commit to.

Kyle and I flew across the US to Boston for several days while I participated in their program. I was able to admit things about myself that I rarely did; I had an overwhelming fear of experiencing low blood sugar, difficulty with exercise because the number of calories I would need to take in to prevent low blood sugar outweighed what I was burning, and stark disconnects from my own body. This team saw my reality for what it was: my health status was not sustainable. I was used to functioning with an average blood sugar of 300, which would lead to serious long-term complications. The goal blood sugars for a type 1 diabetic are between 80 and 180 mmo/L (before and after meals).

At the program, I was able to process these things with other type 1s who related, as well as with counselors and medical professionals who truly specialized in the many facets of managing a complicated condition. While I didn't leave the program with perfect blood sugar, I felt a sense of validation in how difficult managing the disease was, even if you do everything "perfectly."

I became pregnant a couple months after I completed the bootcamp. We were both ecstatic but terrified due to my pre-existing conditions. I saw my endocrinologist regularly to start making changes to my insulin dosing because pregnancy hormones wreak havoc fairly immediately on blood sugars. My A1c (3-month average glucose) dropped from a dangerously high level to a "normal" range due to consistent low blood sugar episodes. While the transition was a good thing for the baby and me, my body went into a shocked state for a few weeks due to living with a high A1c for years prior. I was nauseous, exhausted, and quite shaky. My body accepted very few foods throughout pregnancy; I survived off fruit, yogurt, cream cheese on ritz crackers, sour patch kids, and the occasional bowl of pasta.

Thankfully, I had stepped away from my role at the treatment center to focus on my health, and I was able to stay home, focusing on managing my disease and growing a baby. These somewhat calm and "easier" first few weeks were quickly snubbed by rapid complications for me and our unborn son. After my pregnancy experience, I wrote a lot, partly as a therapeutic process for myself but also for others to read about our journey of prematurity and NICU complications.

This next chapter in the book is a compilation of revised blog posts that I wrote during this time.

ATTICUS

MAY 15, 2017

For the twenty-nine weeks prior to your arrival, my body was fighting. It was fighting hard for both of us to survive. Each day I would wake up unsure of how you and I were going to make it through. Each kick and punch were reminders that despite the very serious medical issues I was facing, you were still where it was healthiest for you. It was hard to describe the fear and guilt I felt; I often questioned whether it was selfish to get pregnant with the known possible risks.

I read hundreds of positive stories of type 1 diabetics experiencing healthy enough pregnancies and birthing full-term babies; I was hopeful that I could too. Unfortunately, this was not my experience despite taking many necessary steps to gain "control" over an often "uncontrollable" disease. All your dad and I wanted was to become parents, and many times throughout my pregnancy, I feared that we were not going to get the chance.

I was about eighteen weeks along when I started the countdown to the number of weeks where you would be considered viable by my medical team. I obsessively researched possible complications for each week of gestation starting from twenty-two weeks onward. The rate of survival and quality of life for premature babies born that early was grim, so I kept praying for more time carrying you. I frequented the emergency room every two to three days due to high blood pressure spikes. For days at a time, I was unable to leave the couch, all I could do was sleep; the exhaustion I felt was deep in every cell in my body. Numerous times throughout the day, I would be flooded with anxiety as my symptoms worsened; the only reassurance I got was the fact that you were still breathing and moving in my tummy.

Starting at twenty weeks, I was finally taken to labor and delivery each hospital visit. They would stabilize my blood pressure, monitor your heartbeat and movement, then send me home. I lost count on the number of times I was taken into triage, only to be repeated seventy-two hours later. Each week that I progressed through the pregnancy, it seemed that I was admitted and kept longer than the previous visit.

At this point, I was seeing the high-risk maternal fetal medicine doctor every week and the kidney specialist every other week due to continued loss of kidney functioning. At the twenty-week growth scan, you were diagnosed with Intrauterine Growth Restriction (IUGR). Each additional concern caused internal separation from myself; dissociation yet again was my greatest coping skill. I wanted to be a mom for as long as I could remember, and despite me "knowing" that the complications weren't my fault, I could not help but feel that it was or that I was making a selfish decision to try to bring you into this world.

I took the thirty-minute drive from our house to the University hospital multiple times a week. The fear I experienced arriving at each appointment was crushing, and I started to doubt my ability to continue going. Slowly, you started dropping on the growth chart, and the doctors explained that the blood flow from your umbilical cord was insufficient for healthy growth and development. Around twenty-five weeks, the realization that you were going to be born soon flooded me with panic, intense guilt, and moments of complete shutdown. I didn't want to be with anyone but you.

MAY 20, 2017

Preparing for your birth and your possible immediate death because of how sick you were was not something I could comprehend. I was hospitalized for the final time in mid-April.

The fluid retention started to affect my organs. It was building up around my heart and chest cavity to the point that breathing was difficult. My kidney function had dropped to stage 3 kidney disease, and my blood pressure was steady at 220/110 while maxed out on medication.

When you're dangerously sick while pregnant, people do not know what to say. Some flooded me with questions, others provided unwanted positivity in hopes of dimming the pain I felt. Surprisingly, some seemed to ignore the seriousness of it, behaving as if I were welcoming a full-term healthy infant.

While in the hospital, I had my blood drawn every four to six hours around the clock. The anticipation of each set of results kept my stomach in my throat. Each knock on my hospital room door sent my nervous system into an activated state. How was I ever supposed to rest while being steadily bombarded by nurses, doctors, medical tests, and interventions? The blue and pink bands around my stomach that detected your heartrate kept me going. If your heart was beating, I could cling onto a sense of hope.

MAY 21, 2017

On April 26, 2017, at 1:45 p.m., you came into this world via emergency C-section. Two days prior to your birth, the doctors came into my room to share that I had progressed to severe preeclampsia, and it was time to induce labor. The medical team was certain that delivering you vaginally was the safest route for both of us. I was flabbergasted that they thought you and I were strong enough for a natural labor. After two days of nonprogressive labor, we decided on a planned cesarean. Several minutes after we had decided to move forward with a planned C-section, the blaring noise of monitors filled my hospital room, and the nurses started moving quickly as panic ensued.

The following few minutes happened so fast. Your heartrate was virtually nonexistent, and they needed to get you out immediately if you were going to survive. The bright lights of the operating room were startling. My eyes were wide, but my body was shaking violently and fighting to stay alert.

Every medical professional was moving fast, too fast for me to track their next move, but I knew it was a life-threatening moment. I started violently heaving over the side of the table. I met Kyle's eyes and saw complete fear and helplessness. My gaze kept moving from Kyle to the doctor who was delivering you, desperately looking for reassurance that you were going to be okay. I vaguely remember the medical team telling me that you were out, but there was no cry.

The medical team was working quickly to stabilize you and me. I had retained several pounds of fluid during my pregnancy, which was overwhelming for the surgical team because they were unsure if I was losing a lot of blood or if it was the fluid; turns out it was both due to a complete placenta abruption.

Kyle stepped away from my side to meet you and take a picture to show me. When I first saw you, I was taken aback at the image of you completely lifeless with a tube down your throat and your skin colorless. Every fiber in my body wanted to hold you and make you better, but I couldn't.

Kyle was so torn on who to stay with; I begged him to go with you and the NICU team. As my medical team worked to stabilize me, I stared at the ceiling, unable to move due to the epidural, unable to speak because of overwhelming fear of not knowing whether you were alive or not; the panic in my chest was heard in my ears.

After I stabilized in the recovery room, I was wheeled to the NICU pod. No matter how many hours of research I had done on being a "preemie" parent, nothing could have prepared us for the emotional and mental anguish of our NICU journey. When I first laid eyes on you, your two-pound body was tucked ever so gently in a curved pillow that was meant to mimic my womb. The tiniest IV and PICC line was placed in your hand and head, and there were several wires going from your body to several different machines next to your incubator. There was a large breathing tube down your throat, connected to a rapidly moving ventilator. You were too fragile to hold, unable to cry because of the breathing tube, and heavily sedated.

Within the first few hours of your birth, I was flooded with waves of guilt. I felt like I had very minimal understanding of how I was supposed to be a mom to a deathly sick child. I relied on Kyle and my mom to sit and gather information as they listened to the doctor discuss the serious medical complications you were facing. As the list of complications grew, so did the deep ache in my heart. I was only allowed to give you a "hand hug" through the incubator, which was light pressure on your body due to how underdeveloped your nervous system was. It wasn't enough.

MAY 24, 2017

About sixteen hours had passed since you were born, and unfortunately, you had not stabilized. A neonatologist came into my hospital room at 5:30 in the morning and woke Kyle and me up. She shared, "Your son is very sick. We do not know exactly what is wrong with him, but you need to come to his room now." My heart literally sank as I panicked to catch my breath and understand the words she was saying. Did she mean you were going to die?

You had only been in this world for a short time, but the list of medical issues that you were facing was too long to comprehend.

Like most people I know, I was naive to the world of premature babies. Despite weeks of research while we prepared for you to come early, I did not fully understand the level of complex medical conditions that premature babies often faced.

My belief in any sort of God started to crumble. I sat in the hard hospital rocking chair, disconnected, watching the large team of doctors and nurses surround your bedside for long periods of time, using medical terminology that was foreign to me. Helplessly, we watched them struggle to keep you stable and alive, the machines constantly beeping and blaring terrifying noises. On day two, you were on the highest level of oxygen support available and using the most powerful ventilator possible. This day felt hopeless, they warned us that if you didn't start improving in your breathing, there was no other medical intervention they could provide you. For a split second, I realized that I may never take you home.

The list of complications you faced was growing: severely premature lungs (respiratory failure), subgaleal bleed in your head, dangerously high blood pressure, severe anemia, and blood that wouldn't clot. The emotional pain I felt was too much to bear at times. It was torturous. How could I be blessed with a baby, born on my sobriety birthday nonetheless, only to have him taken away?

MAY 25, 2017

On the ninth day of your life, we received the devastating news that you had suffered bilateral brain bleeds, an intraventricular hemorrhage (IVH). My ability to breathe was halted. I had read about IVH in one of the preemie books during my pregnancy but had skipped over most of that section because I felt sure that nothing that catastrophic could happen to us. I'll never forget the moment when the young resident came into our cubicle and sat next to me. She started to draw a map of your brain, pinpointing the locations of the bleeds. A sense of hallowing rushed through my body, moving me right into a state of derealization; I was watching myself receive the news from a third-person perspective.

Kyle wasn't there at the time, but one of our primary nurses sat with me while the doctor delivered this latest development, and the expressions on both of their faces conveyed compassion as well as complete uncertainty of what the future held. After the doctor left the room, the nurse stayed and handed me one tissue after another as I sobbed. It was at this moment that I realized that I needed the nurses just as much as you did; they were the experts in caring for severely premature and sick babies, and we were experts in loving you.

Kyle rushed to be with both me and you. For hours, my urge to flee was strong. I paced in our tiny room while trying to shut out the sounds that came from our neighboring infant and the blaring alarms throughout the floor. For the rest of that day, I felt numb, barely speaking to Kyle or anyone. I was flooded with an unwelcome urge to pull away from you because the pain was too great. Why would God give you to us and then take you away?

MAY 30, 2017

Every morning, I stood there among this group of strangers who were your caregivers. They were the doctors and nurses who spoke the complicated language of the neonatal intensive care unit. By then, I was becoming well versed in medical terminology and numbingly adjusted to the constant beeping of the alarms and monitors. Connecting to anyone felt impossible and useless because if I was not going to have you, I didn't want anyone or anything. The vacancy that overtook my body was welcomed and, at times, savored. I was sick of being reminded by others about the importance of taking care of myself during this time; nothing else mattered but you.

I poured hours into researching IVH and the outcomes in babies with the same degree of brain bleeds as you. I read both encouraging and heartbreaking stories; I became obsessed with gathering enough information to accurately predict your future. If I wasn't in action mode, the pain swallowed me whole. Emotional amnesia was the best protective response during this time; the realization of our situation came in and out of focus for the first few weeks. One day, your primary nurse looked at me while I rambled on and on about the research I had done. She interrupted me and asked, "You know he is the same baby today as he was the day before the results came back, right?" Her direct question changed the way I viewed and felt about your health complications. The tiny two-pound baby lying in his incubator was our son regardless of complications we were facing, and I would never change that.

Despite the fears that were still present, my level of acceptance changed for the better, and the out-of-reach expectations I once had for myself, and you disappeared; I felt more confident in being your mom.

JULY 15, 2017

After ninety days in the NICU and a lot of ups and downs, we were able to take you home! While you still required full-time oxygen at home, the disbelief that you were stable enough to be without a 24/7 medical team was great. The realization of having you home was overwhelming due to the unknown of what the future held regarding your growth, development, and health complications, but the excitement overpowered my fears.

I could not believe that you were home. The three of us and our two dogs quickly settled into our new routine. The dogs never left our side when you were in our arms, our cream French bulldog, Bebo, often curled up next to you in your sleeper, and Charlie, my trusted golden retriever, was always at my feet or watching you rock in your swing.

My protective nature was in full force; every fiber of my being would do anything to protect you from getting sick and face another hospital stay. Advocating for our needs as a family was hard for me without coming off too strong and overbearing, which was common for me when communicating my needs.

For the first few months I either found myself emotionally disconnected from how I felt about my pregnancy, birth, and NICU experience, or I became flooded with emotion that I could not describe, often leading to outbursts of disproportionate measure. I would suffer many breakdowns every several weeks without explainable context to those around me. It was like I didn't know why I was feeling the way I did. Other days, flashbacks of lying on the operating table, the nurses resuscitating you, collapsing on the ground in despair, and the times we witnessed you in immense pain flooded my mind. All these memories reminded me of what we almost lost.

THE MISSING PIECE

As Atticus grew and stabilized, we desired to grow our family. As I reflected on my six-week post-birth appointment with the high-risk OBGYN team, the shock of what I was told took time to settle in: I would never be able to carry another child again. I was only twenty-nine years old, and my hopes of becoming a family of five one day was taken away from me. Although none of me wanted to go through what I did during my pregnancy, birth, and NICU stay, Kyle and I desperately wanted more children.

We decided to pursue IVF and gestational surrogacy. A close friend of mine, Courtney, lightheartedly suggested the idea of her carrying a baby for us. Several months later, this turned into our reality. We started the IVF process when Atticus was about nine months old. I had barely physically healed from my traumatic C-section and preeclampsia before beginning the egg retrieval process; patience has never been my strong suit.

In total, we completed three rounds of IVF in less than two years. The daily meds, blood work, and multiple weekly appointments took a toll on me, but nothing compared to the heartbreak of two failed cycles. I "knew" that my body had survived a lot the last several years and had not functioned from a place of homeostasis since before drug addiction and diabetes, but to me, I could do anything if I set my mind to it.

Our first round of IVF was a failure. Kyle and I were walking around downtown Denver after a dinner date when we got the call from the reproductive clinic; none of our embryos were viable. My legs shook, everything around me slowed down, and I felt angry then hopeless. Why was this happening? How could I look Kyle in the eye and tell him more bad news about what my body was not capable of doing? The self-blame engulfed me, and I felt like a failure as a woman.

After the initial shock subsided, we were encouraged to try again by the team at the fertility clinic. They assured us that my eggs were healthy enough. Once my body was in a regular cycle again, we embarked on the second round of IVF. Thankfully, we produced two healthy embryos, one female and one male.

Choosing a woman to replace me as the person who would carry our next baby was an unexplainably difficult decision to make. Kyle and I went back and forth for weeks on whether we wanted someone we knew to carry our baby or a stranger. When discussions with Courtney became more serious, I knew the best decision was to move forward with someone we knew and trusted. I had known since ninth grade; I knew the way she and her partner parented their children, their safe and secure relationship, and the level of calmness she functioned from. To us, it seemed like the perfect environment to foster a pregnancy.

As Atticus grew in his first year, he made immense strides in his emotional and language development, he was still significantly physically behind and dependent on oxygen. Living at the altitude in Denver, CO impacted his ability to breathe without oxygen and unfortunately was setting him back in his respiratory healing. We sold our business and moved back to Arizona but down the mountain from Prescott to Phoenix.

The move was difficult on our family- we left close friends and a city where many 'firsts' happened- our first business and the birth of our first son. I struggled to balance wanting to advance my career and motherhood, Kyle struggled to find a place in the professional landscape after the sale of our business but a few months later secured a position at a medical detox facility.

We moved forward with surrogacy during this in-between time, allowing me to travel back to see Courtney during our surrogacy journey.

We had arranged for the transfer of the embryo to take place close to her home in Lethbridge, Alberta. I flew home to be present for the transfer, and we facetimed Kyle from the procedure room. Our first transfer was a success, and she was officially pregnant. Canada does not allow for gender-specific transfers, so we would all be surprised at the gender reveal.

Despite the overwhelming excitement, I was experiencing confusing and profound feelings of loss related to our baby being in another woman's womb. There were moments of jealousy—her feeling the kicks instead of me, and our baby hearing her voice daily and not mine. I had no one in my life who had been through a surrogacy journey, so I was stuck processing how I felt alone or with random strangers on the internet from support groups.

There were moments when speaking about my feelings felt like I was complaining about this gift we had been given. This was something that I was reminded of several times by well-intended people. Comments such as "Well, at least you don't have to gain weight" or "Good thing you won't have to recover from childbirth or deal with the hormones" stung in a way that no one could understand. I came to believe that more than two things could be true at once. I could hold gratitude for our surrogate and the entire scientific process that allowed it to happen while grieving the loss of my own ability to carry our baby.

Looking for the silver lining is what a lot of people focus on, but unfortunately, the reality of why a silver lining was needed in the first place was left unnoticed by many. I still carried so many painful memories from my pregnancy and the health complications that Atticus and I continued to face. For the twenty-nine weeks I was pregnant with him, I had disconnected from my body completely; the reality of the complications was too hard to comprehend. With surrogacy came another type of separation from the pregnancy.

Despite the on-and-off emotional battle I experienced throughout our journey, the gratitude that we held in our heart for being gifted the utmost precious gift of all was overwhelmingly beautiful. Our baby was in a healthy environment, our carrier was emotionally dedicated to the pregnancy process and birth, and she truly desired to provide a couple with the gift of a newborn.

We found out early in the pregnancy that we were having another baby boy. While my first reaction was an eyeroll (caught on camera) due to being the only female in the house, my heart quickly grew more than I knew possible at the thought of being a mom to two boys.

Courtney's pregnancy was mostly uneventful, with a brief scare in the first trimester and a complication after birth that was quickly attended to. I was able to travel to her several times during the pregnancy, which made me feel a part of the process more. She, Kyle, and I had a group text thread where she would send updates to us about our baby's movements, growth, food dislikes and likes. Atticus and I arrived in Alberta a couple weeks prior to her induction date while Kyle remained at home to wrap up work.

Two days after we arrived, I was woken up by my mom, who stated that Courtney had been trying to call me; her water had broken. Panicking, I called Kyle, trying to arrange how he was going to make it from Arizona to Alberta in time for our son to be born.

As we were checking into labor and delivery, the nurse kept referring to our surrogate as the "mom." My stomach went into my throat and tears welled in my eyes. This simple but impactful statement made by the hospital staff was a reminder that our uniqueness of growing our family was not being truly seen. How come no one was getting this right? I was the baby's mom, not her! I reacted to the nurse in a puddle of tears, subtly demanding she address us properly.

I saw the look in everyone's eye, nudging me to "calm down" and that my emotional reaction was disproportionate to what took place. The feeling of not being seen was looming over me again. Why did I need others to recognize my pain and how difficult this process was for me?

Fortunately, the nurses and doctors assigned to us during delivery were more attuned to the specifics of our situation, and I was involved in all discussions regarding the delivery process while adhering to Courtney's ideal birth plan. Kyle had managed to get on a last-minute flight, but the likelihood of him making it for the birth was decreasing because labor was progressing well. Thankfully, he arrived in the lobby about an hour before our son was born.

I cannot describe the intensity of witnessing my child being born. In that moment, it didn't matter that I wasn't delivering him, only that he arrived safely, and that Courtney was safe too. Once active labor started, the birth happened quickly. Courtney was an absolute rock star, allowing her body to embrace the labor and delivery process without medication, all for another family. This realization left me speechless. After a few pushes, he was out and crying, a sound I had never heard before from a newborn; I didn't hear Atticus cry until he was three weeks old. I cut the umbilical cord, and the nurses placed him on my chest. He looked up at me with his big blue eyes, and in that moment, it was clear that he knew I was his mom. Through science, medicine, and the biggest gift from another family, we were now parents to two boys.

Once Courtney was taken to her own room, Kyle was allowed in to see his son. Before he was born, we questioned how our hearts would expand to love someone else as much as we loved Atticus, but instantaneously it happened, and it was like we had never lived a life without him. We named him Crew Wylder, a name that he truly grew into. He was the most content newborn. He rarely fussed unless it was for food, he was enthralled with his older brother, and he loved snuggles from everyone. We were blessed with almost one month in Alberta, surrounded by my family and our friends while we waited for his birth certificate and passport. A part of me really didn't want to leave. I missed the closest people more than I really knew and honestly dreaded doing "new-born" life again with no family close by.

MOTHERHOOD

While Atticus was still in the most terrifying period of his early weeks and months, my heart was protected from connection because of my guttural fear that he would be taken from me. As he grew out of this early period, I was able to access silliness and emotional lightness around him. I found myself more focused on the health of my spirit and the energy I brought to my home, realizing that this little boy would feel it all. He had already endured a lot of in-utero stress and ninety days of medical trauma in the NICU. I felt a deep sense of responsibility to begin his healing in infancy.

However, I was still experiencing a lot of symptoms related to dissociation and nervous system distress. I struggled a lot to remain oriented to my present-day life when I was not around Atticus; he was my anchor. If I was in mom "mode," it felt like no other emotions were possible to feel and no other actions were possible to take; transitioning from mother to wife and vice versa was glitchy at best. When I was away from Atticus for any period, my wounds were more apparent, and I would often respond to Kyle with very incongruent reactions.

How could I possibly share the biggest responsibility I will ever have with another person and then be their intimate partner? How could I fully trust another person to take care of the little boy who I loved more than life itself? Logically, I could conceptualize why I struggled with these transitions; a lot of people assured me that what I was feeling at times was "normal" and would pass. I came to realize that my loss of control over the emotions I felt and behaviors I acted out with were not "normal"; I was being triggered from my past, and it was greatly impacting my roles in my family. I desperately wanted to be both a loving and secure mother to my son and a supportive, attuned, and intimate partner to Kyle. The integration of these two states, however, felt impossible.

Over time, I started to be able to connect with parts of me that had been hidden since childhood. At some point in my life, I lost the ability to "play" and "be in the moment." This gift was slowly given back to me as my transformation as a mom continued. When things would quiet down and I could be present with our two beautiful blue-eyed boys, my nervous system started to repair, moments at a time. While this type of growth was the most terrifying experience to date, I slowly started to open my heart to it. Allowing myself to experience love and commitment to another human being without a complete overtake by dissociation was deeply changing; I had become a master at guarding my heart over the years.

Throughout Atticus's first two years of life, I was flooded with worry, guilt, and despair about how he may be different from other kids his age. There were glaring differences in his physical abilities. He was fourteen months old and not crawling on all fours and was nowhere close to walking.

For months, I tried to induce positivity and gratitude into what he could do based on the relatively low expectation due to his brain injury, but the gut-wrenching possibility of him having to struggle with disabilities haunted me. I wish I could say that gratitude was enough during this time, but it was not sufficient to calm the inner turmoil that comes with having a sick child.

Kyle did not seem as concerned as I was. He was steadfast in his belief that Atticus would do things on his own time. At times, I was obsessive about the amount of physical and occupational therapy he received. The number of hours I engaged him in exercises outside of scheduled therapy hours was all consuming. As I watched my beautiful, happy little boy enjoy his existence, the panic that swirled through my body on a day-to-day basis was periodically crushing. I struggled to see how engaging, inquisitive, curious, and smart he was sometimes because of the intense panic of what his future could hold.

I started to lose connection with any sort of higher power and certainly my belief in God. I began to question the purpose of such intense struggles. I had done most things right while preparing for my pregnancy: I ate healthy, I exercised, I tested my blood sugar and utilized my insulin pump, but the complications and subsequent trauma still followed me. There were many moments when I asked God why. With no response, my inner narratives insisted I was being punished for treating my body so badly in the past.

When I spoke to others about the reality of my pregnancy, I began to recognize that the way I spoke negatively about it could impact Atticus. I never wanted my trauma narrative to become his inner voice. I started accepting of the importance of addressing the grief and trauma that I felt was stuck inside. I vowed to not discuss the long-term health impacts of my pregnancy in front of Atticus; I never once wanted him to feel that I regretted my pregnancy because not one part of me did. Becoming a mom provided me with the greatest emotional feat, one full of the utmost beauty and deep love coupled with sadness and fear, both changing the way I functioned in my world.

Crew's arrival helped heal some aspects of my pregnancy and birth experience with Atticus as well as expanded my capacity for tenderness. As I watched one of the women who had helped to arrange my intervention many years prior give birth to our son, I was overwhelmed with an emotion I can't define; nothing in the English language can do it justice.

Crew was a special baby, as I am sure every mother and father says, but everyone around him fell in love with his bright blue eyes, his larger-than-life smile, and his intrinsic happiness to just be a part of this world. Crew developed a personality that was so unique to him and immediately drew people in. Everyone he interacted with was taken by his independence, goofiness, and wild and free demeanor. It truly was Crew's world, and everyone else just lived in it.

His daycare caretakers would comment on how he had only one speed and they termed it "Crew speed." They would often call to report minor accidents and bumps and bruises that he received doing something dangerous, none of which was surprising to Kyle and me. He loved exploring his world and what each element had to offer. He loved aggressively and with intent. While he was fiercely independent and stubborn at times, he loved cuddles from mom and dad, intense rounds of being tickled, and acting out every story that was read to him.

I cannot even begin to say how many days we would belly laugh at the outrageous things he would do, like dot paint our cream-colored dog to resemble a dalmatian, take a walk with no clothes on down the block because "he wanted to," color every inch of his body in paint or marker, and make friends with absolutely everyone and everything.

Crew is intense in all areas of his personality, from stubbornness to affection. In public, he would run as if we were in the jungle. He would have his long blond hair flying behind him as he sprinted with no shoes onto his next adventure. Most people would mistake him for a girl due to his angelic face and long hair, even though he was built like a linebacker; they would often shout after us, "Wow, she is fast!" or furrow their brow with judgment.

Boy did we get a lot of parenting suggestions on how to "manage" him and his "behaviors." Most, we sluffed off because many people assumed his wildness was an issue for us, when the reality was, the way he navigated his small world taught us a lot about emotional freedom. I had struggled most of my life with feeling restricted from within, so as I watched my son display the free-spiritedness I had always hoped for, a part of me healed.

Is parenting a wild child challenging? Yes. Is parenting a child with strong self-will frustrating at times? Yes. But the last thing we wanted to do as his parents was quiet down the strong qualities that made him who he was. We never wanted our children to feel that "shrinking" feeling that Kyle and I felt during our own childhoods.

Atticus was a much more stoic and intentional child. He learned to use his mind to understand his surroundings when he was unable to physically explore. He did not learn to walk until the week before Crew was born, when he had just turned two years old. He was observant of his surroundings and of people but formed special bonds to those he trusted and spent time with. He slept on my chest for the first year of his life, oxygen cords and all, soaking in the regulation he desperately needed from my nervous system—and I needed from his.

Being separated from your newborn at birth is not natural, and being denied the gift of holding them for days on end is torturous. Despite the dedication and care of NICU nurses, I do not believe that Atticus received the same care that he would have if he was home with his family. Once we got home, we were determined to heal as many of the attachment misalignments experienced in the NICU as we could. Some would have said that Atticus was "overly attached" to me, but I could never buy into the ideology that a baby could be too reliant on their caregivers. I soaked up every minute I could with him, thanking whatever I believed in for not taking him away from me.

Any expectation I had for the type of mom I was going to be was thankfully altered by parenting two young boys close in age. Truthfully, I imagined I would be a "type A" mom because I was perfectionistic in many areas of my life, but I soon learned to beat to the sound of the drum of Atticus and Crew. When both boys were toddlers, the days were long, but the weeks and months went by too fast. The house was never clean, and the trickeries of little boys ran our lives, but it was hard to complain when their laughter could brighten the toughest day. Nothing made my heart grow larger than witnessing the close bond between them. To this day, they continue to be each other's greatest source of laughter, frustration, and friendship. In many ways, they are inseparable, never wanting to participate in something without one another. And the other times our house resembles the UFC.

When Atticus was an infant and young toddler, his development was unknown, his physical development delayed, but he was always "caught up" with language and cognitive skills. He attended OT and PT services every week, wore a brace on his leg, and was looking at ankle surgery in the future. When he was two years old, he was diagnosed with hemipelagic cerebral palsy, which in his case affected the left side of his body from his core down to the curvature in his foot.

A lot of people in his life were surprised because he didn't "appear" to have a disability or fit their narrative of what cerebral palsy "looked like." While we did not push for a diagnosis, it did validate the difficulties we saw him experience when it came to the left side of his body matching his right. We learned that kids with CP must exert twice as much energy as kids without it to complete a task such as running or climbing; this confirmed our belief that our son was a determined and brave little boy.

Once he reached age three, Atticus seemed to start noticing variances between the way he ran and that of his friends. Witnessing him "feel" different than his friends tore at my heart; I never ever wanted him to be an outcast with other kids, especially starting at a young age. Other kids innocently asked questions about his brace, but once he reached age five, some started to make more direct mean comments. This boiled my blood. We always maintained open dialogue with Atticus about his condition and taught him ways in which he could explain it to others when asked, but only if he felt comfortable.

Learning to balance his desire to not wear his brace and what was medically best for him was difficult; some days I wanted to pretend like his condition didn't exist either, just like he did. Eventually, we decided that the best approach was to focus on his self-confidence development and how to approach difficult interactions with his peers, physical challenges on the playground, and other situations he needed to learn to problem solve in. Once Crew was old enough to run and climb, Atticus's desire to try new things grew.

a new understanding

INTEGRATION

As the months went by, I continued to mostly self-manage my mental health symptoms with sprinkles of therapy in-between. I had read countless articles and books about complex trauma and long-term symptoms. Despite a lot of growth and stability, there were times when I still felt like a puzzle that didn't fit together perfectly.

I had become licensed in the state of Arizona to practice therapy as a licensed clinical social worker and was enjoying being back in the work force. I had cautiously enrolled in an EMDR basic training with several preconceived notions about EMDR, especially because of my personal experience years ago. Prior to this training, I had completed other additional trainings in the treatment of trauma disorders, including Somatic Experiencing, which was the first post-graduate training that resonated with how I experienced myself.

When the facilitator started discussing the long list of cautions before implementing EMDR with complex trauma survivors, my ears perked up. She continued by introducing us to a theory named "Structural Dissociation Theory." As she discussed the nuances of the clinical theory, she used language such as "fragmentation," "parts of the client may have a different perspective," "parts hold memories and sensations related to the trauma," "the system is built for survival," and other key phrases. I experienced parallel emotions of relief and immense fear; this theory described how I felt for years.

For as long as I could remember, I have hated connecting to my body. If I were to connect to it, it would mean that I would have to remember what happened to it. Keeping the sexual abuse experiences separate from me was important, but keeping my body separate from my conscious mind was even more important. I despised every bodily function of the female body. I witnessed many women around me express gratitude and awe for the power of the female body, and while I wanted to cheer them on, I only felt innate revulsion. I hated how our bodies changed with hormone fluctuations, I hated what came out of them, I hated what they did, but most of all, I despised physical responses to sex and intimacy. After intimacy, I would burst into tears and become flooded with self-disgust and shame even after ten-plus years had passed since the last time I was abused sexually. No matter how many ways I was reminded of my current level of safety or my stable marriage with a wonderful man, my body would not stop reminding me of what happened to it.

I read an article once written by a woman who was a sex-trafficking survivor. She matter-of-factly described the number of times she had been raped as 43,200 times in four years. She recalled that every day, approximately thirty different men would rape her; it was hard to comprehend this amount of invasion. With glazed-over eyes, I continued reading the article as if it were a fictional story and not someone's real life experiences. Suddenly, I had a realization about the content of the article; I related to this woman and the emotional state she was in during and after her escape. The number of times that I had unwanted sex was upward of 700 times. When it was over, I would cry with relief that I would get a break from the coercion. I was violated by someone who said they loved me, and even protected me at times. He had introduced me to his family and kids, and frankly, he was someone I was tricked into sharing a life with. Although the "number" of assaults was not near as high and the circumstances different from the woman I read about, her strength became my push to really identify the degree of abuse I had suffered.

As I started to work with more specialized therapists for my own healing, I began to understand my behaviors as the manifestation of a chronically dysregulated nervous system and fragmented psyche. I gained awareness of how out of my "window of tolerance" I functioned. My nervous system was almost always reacting before the logical, frontal cortex of my brain could take over.

I knew that I was a high-functioning, traumatized person. Photos showed me smiling, work knew that I was productive, I was a go-getter and was always inspired to do something new, but I was deeply disconnected from my emotions, memories, and thoughts. There were days and weeks that I floated through my day with minimal connection to anyone or anything. Kyle often asked if I was okay, and I would snap back telling him that I was. I couldn't stand to explore the internal chaos of my mind and body. While the harsh words slipped out of my mouth without control, a protective barrier was automatically in place; I had no idea how to explain the truth to him and didn't want to.

When my therapist started to treat my symptoms through a lens of structural dissociation theory, I was slowly able to make sense of my dissociation and my contrasting emotional responses. The integration process of my dissociative processes was painful because I went from believing these things didn't happen to me to feeling and knowing that they did. I also learned the narrative behind many distressing somatic symptoms, which was startling. While many clients I've treated as a professional were able to describe more detailed parts of their personality—including ages and "versions" of self, mine showed up as nervous system states. These nervous symptoms states governed the way I felt in this world, how I felt unsafe in a safe relationship, why I felt terrified that someone was always going to hurt me, the inclination that I was being watched, and the disgust I felt toward my own body.

My go-to response to something or someone being "too much" was to flee, in whatever way I could; the alarm bells went off and I needed out. While I rarely physically fled a situation, the way I "went away" was dissociation. My system struggled to tolerate any sense of overwhelm, danger, and shame. The threads of those feelings interweaved into the physical, sexual, and emotional abuse as well as the presenting medical distress. Regardless of being able to separate my current self from what happened in the past, my brain and body held onto the shock of the events.

SLIPPED AWAY

During this time, my best friend in sobriety was slipping away from me with mental health symptoms and active addiction. She tried more than anyone I knew to stay sober: constantly attending AA meetings, repeating the steps over and over, and helping people get sober. Kelsey was the one to introduce me to the beauty of long-term sobriety at that meeting over ten years ago, she was the first one I related to wholeheartedly. Yet between 2016 and 2021, her struggles to maintain stability in her marriage and her role as a mother, employee, and daughter were overpowering.

For short and sometimes long periods of time, I saw her face full of relief and happiness again. I saw how much she was enthralled with her two little girls and how dedicated she was to getting better. But other times, I didn't even recognize her; the words that came out of her mouth sounded like a different persona, her behavior shocked me, and the desperation for more substances caused a knot so tight to form in my chest I could barely breathe.

During this period, many people Kyle and I got sober with were in pain. Some relapsed and others were overtaken by mental health disorders. I struggled to understand why others around them advocated for their attendance at AA only—no suggestion of mental health treatment, no therapist or psychiatrist intervention, just pure peer-to-peer support in the basement of a church.

In March 2021, Kyle, the boys, and I were boarding a plane to Hawaii for a family vacation. As we tried to wrangle the boys in their seats before takeoff, my phone text messages went off. I glanced at it was a text from Kelsey's brother: *"Hi Chels, I'm sorry to have to say this but we found out kels passed away today."*

A loud gasp left my mouth, and Kyle turned around from the seat in front of me. My eyes were filled with tears immediately, the shock overwhelming. I couldn't speak, so I handed him my phone so he could read the text message for himself. Overhead, the pilot said, "Please prepare for takeoff and ensure your electronics are put in airplane mode."

I used my phone for as long as I could until my service shut off above 10,000 feet. Silent tears poured from my eyes for hours. My heart was broken.

As my tremendous loss sunk in more, the distain I had for AA grew. I was concerned for the people, like Kelsey, who needed greater mental health intervention through their sobriety journey instead of the continuous redirection back to a twelve-step meeting.

For the first time, I saw the program as an organized structure that had the potential to cause a lot of harm.

A NEW FREEDOM

After several years of "parts work" through a structural dissociation lens, I was introduced to Deep Brain Reorienting (DBR). This approach allowed me to turn toward feelings, experiences, and memories in a more tolerable way than EMDR did. The approach targeted the deepest level of the nervous system—instead of targeting the trauma itself, the felt sense of turning toward or turning away from something threatening or painful was chosen as the activating moment.

As we processed through various "targets" at the deep brain stem level, the survival responses I had, slowly discharged from my body. My legs would shake, my body would vibrate. Unknowingly, I would turn toward sensations in my body representing being trapped, whether that was on the surgery table or on a dirty mattress. Despite moments of dissociation trying to interrupt processing during a session, DBR does a beautiful job of moving underneath dissociation in the brain to the core shock of the trauma. My body began to connect to itself in a way I did not expect. For the first time, I made intentional contact with the unpleasant, the ickiness, and the unbearable in my body; this was something I could never get to before without serious dissociative processes stepping in and protecting my adult self.

Working from the bottom up eventually led to my behaviors changing. I wasn't in a perpetual state of hypervigilance, I stopped yelling as often, I stopped running from the vulnerable connection required in my marriage, and my tendency to jump into protective mode became less frequent.

While my symptoms felt more understood by Kyle and those closest to me, I was still challenged by having to mask and "pretend" with certain people and in specific dynamics. I also could feel myself falling back on unhealthy coping skills or behavioral traits when around groups of people who didn't feel completely safe. I could sense a narcissist from across the room and became hyper-attuned to my environment, scared of that person's behaviors—even if I didn't know them. If I was scared or overwhelmed, I would shrink into myself and often flee as quickly as possible. I miraculously learned to find safety within myself at first, just not with others.

With friends, family, and previous therapists, I had never had the words to describe how I felt or the processes in my mind. Most of the time when I would describe my "forgetting" or "lack of memory" to others, the assumption was that I used mental health as an excuse for lack of accountability. The few times I attempted to describe the internal dialogue that went on in my mind (what I now know are "dissociative parts" of the personality) or the visual and auditory hallucinations that were intense flashbacks, I was met with a puzzled tone and confused expression. Gaining an actual understanding of the validity of my symptoms and the fact that dissociative disorders are highly underdiagnosed, misunderstood, and mistreated validated my previous clinical experiences.

While therapy didn't wipe away the symptoms like the trauma didn't happen, it softened me; my inner criticism, shame, and self-rejection lessened. I remembered more of my past but from an adaptive standpoint. I came to recognize most things that had happened to me, actions I had taken, and ways in which I had harmed others because of my unhealed wounds. I began to move toward a "healed enough" place.

Throughout these years of complex and layered healing, I experienced something that for years I didn't think I could survive. My phone dinged over and over with screenshots of a GoFundMe account that had been posted that morning. My ex had died.

This event stirred a tangle of emotions: relief, numbness, and gratitude. Internally, I was relatively quiet, relieved by the realization that someone who used to hold so much power of over me would never have the chance to hurt me or anyone else again.

Curiosity got the best of me over the next few days, and I followed the story as it unfolded on social media. The messages posted by other women, declaring their appreciation for him always making them feel on top of the world by adorning them with compliments and charm took my breath away. Were they raving about the same man who sexually abused many women throughout his life? Instead of being flooded with uncontrollable confusion like I would have been years prior, I quickly settled into my truth: I was fully aware of what he did to me, how horrifically painful, humiliating, and cruel his actions were and that what happened wasn't because I was bad and gross. I had reached a place of realization in a way that others in his life hadn't, especially the women he had been with or was with currently.

A breath of gratitude filled the air.

THE BODY CATCHES UP

It took me until I was in my early thirties to fully realize and accept that I was chronically ill. Since being diagnosed with type 1 diabetes, there had been many moments that I was forced to see the consequences of the disease, but they were quickly bypassed as a single "event" that was made worse from type 1.

If I accepted that I was chronically ill, it would mean two things, that I didn't have any control (again) over what happened to my body, and I would have to slow down and ask for help. Each time I got sick with a typical virus that others around me could fight off, it became clearer how difficult of a time my body had; I often ended up in the hospital with dangerously high blood sugar. Prior to getting clean and sober, my diabetes care was less than acceptable. It had been downright dangerous, so I assumed that getting sober would drastically improve it. While I was not as careless as before, I lacked the confidence, connection to my body, and discipline to effectively treat the disease.

Many people assumed that I didn't care enough about my health or did not know how to manage the disease, neither of which were true. I obsessed about my blood sugar stability every day, probably to a fault. The number of secret tears I shed when my bloodwork would come back and show a high A1C matched the number of fibs I told my family and Kyle regarding my blood sugar management. I couldn't bear the idea of letting them all down.

Over the years, I had developed many different ideas about what I needed to stabilize my blood sugar; one was for

Kyle to hound me daily about taking the right amount of insulin; another was to find the perfect endocrinologist, the perfect therapist, or follow the suggestions of people in AA and complete the twelve steps around the disease. Time after time, I was let down by my attempts. The hopelessness I felt had to be tucked away into a safe that no one held the key to.

I actively avoided the notion that I should attend therapy to address being chronically ill, and it seemed to be not on anyone else's radar. I was afraid that if I opened the wound, it would be too big and too painful to manage. Holding a conversation with anyone regarding type 1 besides others with type 1 produced either instant tears or immediate righteous anger.

The mental gymnastics my brain did surrounding type 1 was interesting. If I felt that someone was telling me what to do or making ridiculous suggestions about the disease, I would immediately become defensive and advocate for myself. If people ignored the fact that I had type 1 or dismissed the difficulty of managing it, my throat would tighten and I was overcome with a sense of shrinking, like my lived experiences weren't valid. I started to view my disease like a piece of luggage that I had to drag along with me. I refused to make it a part of me.

A NEW SUFFERING

Right after Crew was born, I started to experience sharp, quick, stabbing on the left side of my head and face. The pain was jarring, but the episodes were brief, so I shrugged them off for several months. As time went on, the frequency and duration of the pain increased. I saw a handful of neurologists who wanted to throw medication at me to treat "migraines" despite minimal migraine symptoms. I felt unheard by those around me on the severity of the pain. I was told countless times to take Tylenol and Advil or sit in a dark room, none of which made a dent in the pain. It was so intense, the pain radiated throughout my cheek, nasal cavity, ear, cheekbone, roof of my mouth, and jaw, bringing me to my knees, hyperventilating.

I experienced such poor care in the neurology clinics I went to that I joined several different facial pain Facebook groups to gain support and information. After several trips to the ER, multiple medical journals read, and connection with countless others who suffered similarly, it was concluded that I suffered from cluster headaches, also known as "suicide headaches."

As I entered this era of medical challenges, I did not know how I would survive. The episodes increased to daily and then multiple times a day. I would scream, sob, rock back and forth, and fight the urge to bang my head against the wall. The helplessness was overpowering, and for the first time since I was a teenager, I started to experience passive suicidality at the possibility of the pain never going away.

I had no idea how to make it through the day. This disorder started to gravely impact my ability to show up as a mother, wife, and an active participant in day-to-day activities. I hated showing people the level of pain I was in, I told myself many times that it was not acceptable to complain about the suffering I was experiencing because others had it worse. I questioned myself on a consistent basis whether I was making it out to be more than it was, which was a similar maladaptive skill that I had used most of my life.

After I joined the support groups online, I started to really recognize how rare this headache condition was and that the only people who would truly ever understand were fellow sufferers. I discovered that while many of my symptoms were like those of others, some did not match the traditional diagnostic screening and started to lead me in another direction.

I had been experiencing the severe pain for almost four years when I met a neurosurgeon who saw something on my MRI. It took a while to properly assess its entirety, but I felt closer to having facts about my disorder. Not only did I have a bone growth that was compressing my trigeminal nerve, but I also had several pieces of bone calcification that had broken off and were floating throughout the nerve toward my brain; leading to an additional diagnosis of Trigeminal Neuralgia. The occurrence of these phenomena happening together were even more rare than the disorders themselves. While the findings complicated my diagnosis even further and left me without a primary one, I was relieved that a medical test showed something to account for the severity of my pain.

Simultaneously, my kidney function was decreasing exponentially. I had stage 4 kidney disease, which was one step away from complete kidney failure. The panic that ensued when the reality would sink in felt unmanageable, and therefore, it was better tucked away. Being faced with a life-or-death diagnosis was something I could never accept;

the actuality of it was too scary. I knew for certain that I did not want to die and leave my boys without a mom, my husband without a wife, and my family and friends without me. I had worked endlessly to heal from addiction and trauma and could not comprehend life being taken from me under medical circumstances.

Most days, I could not access my medical reality. I remained in a de-realized state and lived as if I weren't inching closer to death. Despite the chronic pain and daily extreme exhaustion, my strongest desire was to be an active mother, wife, and friend; my ability to "outperform" my diseases was inconceivable to some but understood by those who knew me well. Like previous trauma I had experienced, some days I would get hit hard with the actuality of my circumstances and explode with deep emotional pain. Other times, I would stay safely in a state of derealization. The stress from this up and down pattern wrecked any hope of blood sugar stabilization, which only further decreased my kidney functioning. The vicious cycle felt inescapable.

THE FIGHT

If I had learned anything along the way about chronic illness, it was the importance of self-advocacy. My determination and fight involving medical care increased exponentially when I had Atticus. It was second nature to fight for my baby. He was my only purpose during those first several months. Thankfully, this fight started to flow into my own complex medical needs. While my behaviors were very task oriented, emotionally void actions, it helped propel me forward into a world-renowned hospital for organ transplant.

I saw a nephrologist every three months to continue assessing my decreasing kidney function. The feedback and support I received was always underwhelming, leaving me feeling more alone, uncertain of the future, and confused about the severity of my condition. Their professional advice was, "We will continue to monitor you as you move closer to dialysis," with no suggestion of searching out a transplant program.

To combat the lack of support I received from professionals, I started researching the parameters around kidney transplants and discovered that "preemptive" (pre-dialysis) transplants were offered at specific transplant programs and included the possibility of a pancreas transplant too. Due to the lack of guidance that I was receiving from my current nephrologist, I decided to self-refer to a top transplant program in the country. I had learned that self-advocacy in the medical system was a necessity because it was designed for patients to deteriorate drastically before intervention would take place.

As I reflect on the process, I lack memory of the referral process and what steps I took. I went into hyper-independence with completion of tasks that, at times, didn't even feel like mine. Fully connecting to the reality that I was going to die without dialysis or a transplant felt too daunting to comprehend. It would hit me full force when I least expected it, and the emotions related to possibly leaving my kids was too much to process, so I separated from it and continued with daily living.

In December 2023, I was accepted into the preemptive transplant program. While I had a complex medical history, there was good news, after days of testing and medical assessments, the rest of my organs were deemed healthy enough for the surgery. The challenging news was I had to gain "control" over my headache and facial pain disorders with neurology prior to being actively listed for transplant. This parameter meant a difficult neurosurgery in my near future.

Once I conceded to the degree of pain I was in and accepted it as mine, it became more overwhelming to deal with; I had done a relatively phenomenal job for years, forgetting each episode after it ended. Nearly no one in my life knew about the chronic pain outside of my closest friends and family. Besides my worried parents, it was rarely a topic of conversation with anyone.

As I waited for a plan from neurosurgery, I started to frequent the ER just to survive that day. I had no method of managing the pain at home because there were virtually no medical interventions I could use without damaging my kidneys further. Advocating for myself at the emergency room was a new form of self-advocacy. Since both disorders were rare, few doctors and virtually no nurses had ever heard of either Cluster Headaches or Trigeminal Neuralgia. I quickly became used to hospital staff not believing me, treating me like I was seeking opiates, or having no clue how to manage my case. These experiences took me right back to questioning my reality or raging with injustice.

The term "medical gaslighting," which was introduced to me through my support group, is when a healthcare professional dismisses or invalidates a patient's concerns or symptoms without an explanation. My mind replayed like a rolodex, flashes of doctors' appointments, hospital stays, and a hollowness in my core when recognizing how many medical specialists treated me this way; endocrinologists, nephrologists, gynecologists, and neurologists were all included in the list. I was finally connecting why I often left my appointments feeling deflated and unable to be helped.

While chronic sexual abuse and domestic violence were different traumas in comparison to medical trauma, my nervous system responded similarly; often with the reaction or state that felt the safest. I oscillated between being flooded with the certainty of my medical state or completely shut off to the idea or suggestion that I was chronically ill. I hesitated to share my conditions with most people in my life, while those closest to me knew more than others, the actual lived daily experience was left for Kyle only or the lucky family members and friends who stayed with us for a longer period. I had become an expert in separating myself from the pain and the secondary symptoms that came with it: the exhaustion, the deepening depression, and the life-altering anxiety. I felt that if I were to become too close or more realized to my symptoms, I would be swallowed whole and never return to a functioning state.

DESTABILIZED

I officially completed the transplant program testing in January 2024. My neurosurgery was booked for March of that year, and then I could be listed as active on the transplant list. The wait for neurosurgery was unbelievably challenging due to the level of pain I experienced daily. Every single day, I was desperate for some relief. Each episode led me to think, "I cannot possibly continue living like this." I was passively suicidal every single day, solely due to the degree of the pain I was in. The despair, sadness, and sounds that would come out of me during an attack were horrific; it was startling to everyone around me, especially my kids. I started to really resent my own body, feeling like a burden to those around me.

The moments in between the attacks of pain, I wholeheartedly enjoyed life. I was honestly happy; our boys were thriving in school and activities, Kyle and I were in a stable and content place in our marriage, our business was growing and helping people heal. Despite my incredibly challenging medical diagnoses, I wanted and believed in my future and our future as a family. The suicidal ideations were fleeting and only arose when the pain hit. Most people who met me had no idea how sick I was. In fact, when I begrudgingly shared my medical status, especially to others in the field of mental health, they were shocked and often speechless.

I had a lot of hope for the microvascular decompression surgery (MVD). I was seeing one of the top neurosurgeons in the country at Mayo Clinic. A couple weeks prior to surgery, I had to get a CT scan of my head and brain. The results were less than ideal. I had a large overgrown bone that was compressing on my trigeminal nerve and bone calcification floating throughout the length of the nerve, toward my brain stem. The procedure was not straightforward like typical MVDs; in fact, my surgeon could only find one other case in medical journals that mimicked mine. It was easy after this to question why—why me, why my family, and why my body. I rationally knew I wasn't being punished for how I lived my life prior to getting sober, but in difficult moments, it felt like that. Between type 1 diabetes, kidney failure, the headache and facial pain disorder, as well as my ongoing healing from mental health symptoms, I felt overcome with hurdles just to live a life that was "stable enough."

The morning of surgery, Kyle and I drove to Mayo Clinic. We were anxious but hopeful. The medical team had communicated to me that I would be in pain when I woke up, but it should be tolerable with pain medication; according to them, most patients wake up and are eating within a few hours. As they prepped me for surgery, butterflies (not the good kind) started to form in my stomach and anxiety of the unknown took over. Kyle was sitting at my bedside, and I could tell that he was scared, our nervous systems in sync.

The pre-op nurse stated that she was going to insert an IV, but first she had to numb my arm due to the size of needles required for a neurosurgery; this kickstarted the realization that I was about to get my skull sawed open. The neurosurgery and anesthesiology team came into my bay and described to me how they would keep me stable in the ER during the six-to-eight–hour surgery and the steps that the surgeon would take to remove the bone and calcification from my brain. I started to drift, the room became blurry, the words spoken from the doctors' mouths seemed further away, and I was overwhelmed with fear while reiterating to my family and friends that I was "ready."

"Chelsey, Chelsey, can you hear me, Chelsey?" Next came a flash of bright light and the most intense pain I had ever felt, then things went black.

This was my experience for the first forty-eight hours after the surgery. I imagined this was like being in coma. I could hear those around me talking but could not engage or move; I was trapped in my body. I recall deeply regretting the surgery, scared I would never come out of the state I was in. Every time I attempted to move my head, I threw up, the most painful heaving one could physically experience. I have flashes of visitors coming, my dad, stepmom, and Kyle—but they felt a million miles away, I couldn't tolerate a touch or even whisper from them without my surroundings disappearing into a dark hole.

I ended up in diabetic ketoacidosis in the hospital due to the mismanagement of my type 1 by the nursing staff, ending me back to the ICU. I couldn't lift my own head, let alone my entire body, so I remember them using a hospital lift to transfer me from bed to bed. I never once thought I would be this helpless at this point in my life.

On the third day post-surgery, I was able to open to my eyes and slowly orient to those around me. I saw my dad and Kyle sitting in my hospital room, both engulfed in both worry and relief to see me open my eyes. The first time I reached for my phone, I saw over two hundred notifications. I instinctually called my mom, and I heard her breathe a deep sigh of relief and say, "It is so good to hear your voice." It was then that I realized how serious my situation had been.

Despite the trauma of the first few days, I still clung to hope that the surgery had been successful. I had yet to feel the unbearable pain that I had prior to surgery. After the post-op pain settled, I was TN pain free for eight solid weeks, which was a gift I would not give back. Despite the initial success, the familiar shocks, burning, and intense pressure started to come back; I didn't say a word to anyone for weeks. Not only was the condition traumatic to me, but it was also traumatic for people who spent any substantial amount of time with me.

Months after the surgery, the pre-surgery pain was officially back, and this time, it started peaking its ugly head on both sides of my face. How could this happen? Why couldn't my already rare condition rest where it was rather than increasing the "rareness" and developing on both sides? The unanswered "why" plagued me and my doctors. Bilateral trigeminal neuralgia pain was rare, only inflicting about 0.5–5 percent of cases.

About three months after my brain surgery, I slowly made my way back to the neurosurgeon's office with my head down. We all knew the surgery was a risk due the complexity of the anatomy in that area of my skull and brain, but I felt the universal disappointment throughout the surgeon's office.

My medical team was focused on my kidney function and getting me listed as active on the transplant list. It was like everyone checked the mark on the to-do list prior to transplant without ever checking the actual status of my head and face pain, which still controlled my days.

As Kyle and I sat down in my nephrologist's office to review my latest lab work for my kidney function, every ounce of my body vibrated with anxiety. He held my hand, and I reluctantly accepted. Any type of physical touch and connection from him often broke down the barrier I put up in my medical appointments, one that allowed me to see myself from a third-person perspective. My old defense strategies of dissociation and disconnection failed me in this moment as I watched the words "We must prepare for dialysis" come out of the doctor's mouth. I broke down into heavy sobs, emptying the doctor's Kleenex box and avoiding eye contact with anyone in the room.

I fought to pay attention as she explained the potential complications of dialysis because all I could think of was our boys. What would this next phase in my medical journey do to them? The doctor wasn't shy in reminding us that dialysis was not a cure for kidney failure, only a treatment that not everyone's body could tolerate. I wanted her to stop talking. My body was overheating and my mind racing; I winced at every image that popped into my head about what my future would look like.

The doctors shared with me the differences between hemodialysis and peritoneal dialysis and my candidacy for each. Both carried their own set of risks, logistical concerns, and more. Due to previous abdominal surgeries and a large amount of scar tissue in my stomach from a life of type 1 diabetes, peritoneal was most likely off the table.

I underwent a surgery shortly after this to place a fistula in my arm for hemodialysis, which is the port of entry where I would be poked and hooked up to a machine at least three times a week at a dialysis center. Each round of dialysis would take anywhere between four and six hours. I would be stationary as the machine recycled and cleaned the blood in my body since my kidneys were no longer doing that job.

My stomach churned and my logical mind kicked on. How would I ever manage a busy career, my kids, marriage, animals, and a home while being tied to a machine up to eighteen hours a week? I had always strived to be a stable parent, and my health complications were threatening this. My entire family system was being affected by something that none of us could control; we were destabilizing.

The internal management that was required to maintain status quo was grueling. My dissociative symptoms really kicked up. I had to be separate from the overwhelm and panic that took over every single day. To all outsiders, I lived a typical life, busy with a young family and career. Not many people were invited to my bear witness to my health struggles, not only due to my own privacy desires but because the more I discussed it, the more real they would become.

WAITING FOR A NEW LIFE

I was officially listed on the transplant list in May 2024. When I received the letter in the mail, I barely glanced at it. I could not comprehend that at thirty-six years old I was going to die without the gift of new organs from a stranger who would, heartbreakingly, lose their life first. The period between being actively listed and receiving a call for organs was one of the most anxiety-ridden times in my life and my family's. Every single time the phone rang, my heart skipped a beat, especially if it was from a number I did not know. The transplant coordinator instructed me to "never be away from your phone" and "have it on you anyplace you go." If you miss a call, you have thirty minutes to return their call or else the organs will be offered to someone else.

My first call came the morning we got back from a week away in California, our favorite summer escape from the Arizona heat. I was towel drying my hair after a shower when my phone rang. It was a transplant coordinator with an "organ offer." These offers are complex and require a lot to go "right," which is difficult to acknowledge considering someone must die "in time" or in the "right way" for organs to be viable. It all depended on factors such as whether the donor is on life support, the window of time for donor to pass after life support is removed, and the evaluation of the organs after they are removed from the donor and harvested. Disappointingly, the call that came in ten hours after the initial "offer" call was to let me know that the pancreas was not viable for transplant.

I had only been listed as active for seven weeks after being told the wait time was going to be approximately twelve months, leading to a mix of excitement and trepidation. We were not expecting the two additional calls that took place within the same week. The heartache that my family and I experienced each time the transplant team said "We have to cancel the surgery due to pancreas not being viable" was heavy. We cried for me and for the donor's loss of life and their family.

It is hard to put into words the mental gymnastics that happens during the process of waiting for a transplant. For me and my loved ones, there was a desperation that the organs were healthy enough for transplant, but it was also impossible to not recognize the grief that another family was experiencing; it felt like a cruel trick that the world was playing on both the donors' family and mine.

When I received the third call, I was admitted to the hospital, pre-surgery testing done, eleven vials of blood drawn—by all accounts I was ready. Kyle brought the boys to say goodbye to me. It was our last moment as a family before our world hopefully changed for the better. I sat in the hospital bed, a familiar place for me, anxiously waiting for the transplant team to come in and wheel me back. The door to my room opened and it was the surgeon; he was there to deliver the bad news. The surgery was not happening. I packed up my hospital bag and we drove home heartbroken. The boys were confused about why I was going home. While they were happy, I could tell that they were starting to grasp the reality that I needed the surgery to "get better."

This last failed offer sent me into a state of chronic panic. Each moment it felt like I was gasping for air. I was either pacing or shut down. It felt like I had no resilience left. The transplant team kept reminding me to "stay strong for transplant" and that "it will happen when it's meant to." The last statement made me question my own morality and that of others. If I received organs when I was "meant to," did that mean that the donor was "meant" to die that day?

Two days after the third call, my fourth call came in, and it was the one. They called with an "offer," I accepted it and was then told to arrive at the hospital within two hours. The only information I was given about the donor was that they were under eighteen years old and male. My stomach went into my throat with the realization that my life was being saved because someone so young lost their life. My entire body was vibrating from the inside out as I repacked my hospital bag, taking deep breaths to steady myself.

I immediately updated my family text thread that was titled "hope, courage, and love." My parents and stepparents had discussed behind the scenes who would come out first, and it was decided that both my mom and dad would; they booked an immediate flight. At around 11:30 p.m., Kyle and I said our goodbyes, and I drove to the hospital alone. There was no one to stay with our kids, one of the downsides of living in another country away from guaranteed support. Kyle was drained of all color when I was preparing to leave him and the kids. I entered the boy's room while they slept. I kissed them goodbye and prayed to the universe that I would get to see them again.

I checked into the hospital with overwhelming nervousness, anxiety, and excitement. The donor surgery was delayed due to bad weather impacting the transplant team's travel to the deceased. The donor surgery had started at 9:30 p.m., and we got notified that the organs were officially accepted at 10:51 p.m. Due to more weather delay in transporting the organs back to my hospital, my surgery was delayed from 2:00 a.m. until 4:00 a.m.

It was the middle of the night when I was wheeled down into pre-op. The room was sterile, white, and completely silent besides the beeping of machines attached to me. I was the only patient in the area, though a nurse was there, trying to keep me company with small talk while we waited. Once the transplant team gave the go-ahead that the organs were ready for transplant, my ability to stay connected to myself was fading. I was too terrified to connect to what felt like indescribable emotions. I quickly sent text messages to the people closest to me, letting them know that I was being wheeled back into the operating room.

Nine hours later, as I blinked my eyes to open, it hit me. I was alive. It was then that I saw Kyle, and I was flooded with gratitude. I eagerly tried to speak, but instantly gagged because I had a tube in my nose that went down my throat. My happiness started to fade as I realized the state of my body: tube down my nose, large IVs in multiple areas, a central line, tubes through my stomach, and a massive incision splitting my stomach down the middle that throbbed.

The first few days in the hospital after the transplant went relatively smoothly. My pain was managed, I had an appetite, and I was engaging with everyone who visited. I wore a continuing glucose monitor for a few days and watched as my blood sugar responded "normally" to everything I ate. It felt like the blueprint of what made up my body started to shift. I started with small steps in my hospital room, walking from my bed to the bathroom, and eventually, I was able to venture out and take laps around the unit with my walker. Some days I was overly adventurous and took the elevator downstairs to the cafeteria. I wasn't allowed to touch anything or breathe without a mask covering my face. The doctors explained that I was so immunocompromised the first several months after transplant that any type of germs could have severe consequences.

Each time my bloodwork results came back while in the hospital, showing a working kidney and pancreas, I was flooded with disbelief. I saw the tears in my parents' eyes, and I could tell that they felt a degree of gratitude that wasn't explainable; their daughter's life had been saved. The debilitating fear of death that had encased me prior to the transplant shifted to a cautious mindset. We were all aware that complications and rejection were looming possibilities, but despite those fears, I started to develop a small sense of hope that this second chance at life was really happening.

I underestimated the power of high-dose steroids. There was a false sense of "superwoman" that overtook me in the hospital but dramatically fell away when I got home. The low blood pressure disabled me from walking from my bed to the bathroom or be self-sufficient with the easiest task.

My hemoglobin was extremely low, wiping out any energy stores I had; I felt like I was in an igloo for weeks, shaking violently as my body struggled to warm itself. I lost over twenty pounds in three weeks as I struggled to nourish my body at all. I saw the fear in my family's eyes, especially on my kids' faces. My heart broke when I attempted to see myself through their eyes. How was it for them to see their mother so incapable of taking care of them, let alone herself? There were several nights where we all piled into bed and cried; the agony of the mental and physical trauma was felt by all of us.

In addition to my parents, my best friends from Canada and Wisconsin traveled to Scottsdale over the next six weeks to help care for me, local ones too. One by one, they took turns being my caregiver, helping with the house, and spending time with our boys; I am forever indebted to my cheerleaders and greatest supports.

Despite these moments of complete agony, a remarkable thing happened, I started to connect to what my body was going through. I became interested in where my new organs had been placed, something I could not tolerate learning about prior to the surgery. I was more present with my body than I had been in years. As the number of days multiplied where I experienced normal blood sugar levels, the cells that made up my body felt healthier and more alive. I no longer felt poisoned from the toxins that had built up in my body because my new kidney worked better than my originals had in years. Fun fact: during a simultaneous kidney and pancreas transplant, they keep the original organs in and place the new ones at the front of your body cavity.

As the initial several weeks passed, I slowly gained some strength back. My desire to return to full-fledged functioning state knocked me on my ass a few times. I had to accept that it wasn't possible yet. My strength was virtually nonexistent the first few months' post-transplant, and my stamina was very short lived. I was desperate to be an active caregiver in my boy's lives again, not their mom who had to stay on the sidelines.

Despite the hardship, the entire transplant process continues to reshape me. There's a deepened sense of purpose, a stronger connection to my body, and a new outlook on life—but there are also scars, visible and invisible, that linger.

4 MONTHS LATER

I lay on a hospital bed for a routine biopsy on my new organs. Against my request, they keep you awake for this procedure. As the doctors tried to numb my stomach with lidocaine, I insisted it wasn't working. I could feel each deeper layer they stuck a needle into. Tears streamed down my face as they released the metal tool used to capture a piece of my new organs, one by one, the pain radiating throughout my abdomen. I was in between being connected to what was happening and leaving reality, drifting somewhere into the ceiling of the room. A nurse gently touched my leg for assurance, and it shocked me back into the moment. I started to sob out of sadness and anger. Why did she have to connect with me?

It was then that I recognized there was more deep work to be done about my medical trauma, past and ongoing. The healing continues.

This biopsy showed mild pancreas rejection. I felt my eyes gloss over, and brain turn away from the doctor's words. They assured me that with treatment, it should resolve. The treatment was high dose steroids that were done via IV in the infusion center at Mayo clinic. I had visited the infusion center multiple times since transplant to treat severe anemia that was leading to profound weakness; it felt like that door had closed behind me and now, I had to reopen it for a short time.

While there was not a follow up biopsy, my medical team examined my biweekly labs to assure my new pancreas was functioning well; after a few weeks I was cleared from risk of acute rejection.

As my energy continued to increase, while unpredictable at times, I felt pieces of myself returning. At first it was more subtle, waking up in the morning and not wanting to go back to sleep, being able to drive my kids to and from school, walking a further distance without being out of breath. One day the realization struck hard, I was no longer living with Type 1 diabetes. My body wasn't bound to insulin pumps and blood sugar crashes. I wasn't drowning in kidney failure symptoms anymore, waiting for them to completely give out.

I was in shock every day that my body was functioning without betraying me. I always had a plethora of bucket-list items I looked forward to, but when I was sick, I could feel them slipping away. Receiving new organs allowed these dreams to come back into focus, and I have slowly started inching toward them; finishing this book was near the top of the list.

My life has taken me to some dark lows—many of them a great threat to my mental health, physical safety, daily functioning, and most recently, my life. The healing I have done throughout the last fifteen years has led me to be the mom I am today, a wife who is able to make space for connection, a friend who doesn't take advantage, a sister who is loving and reliable, and a daughter who is honest, helpful, and forthright.

I am healed enough to maintain a life better than I could have ever expected.

healed enough

The dual organ transplant did not simply give me new organs; it gave me an opportunity to start rebuilding a life that for a long time had seemed completely out of reach. Yet even with a second chance at life, I still carry with me echoes of the hospital rooms, the beeping of my hospital machines, the anesthesia-laced flashbacks, and the suffocating grip of helplessness and fear. I am learning to balance the reality of having healthy transplanted organs with the fear that they could fail at any point; both can be all consuming truths. The medical trauma is not only etched into my body as physical scars but into my nervous system. Being close to death impacted me just like the traumatic events from childhood, adolescent years, and adulthood; they all feel interwoven into one sometimes.

I still suffer from trigeminal neuralgia and different types of head/facial pain. I have continued to work with a neurosurgery and neurology team to find the best treatments for my case, but progress has been very limited.

My work of healing from complex trauma has not been linear. I would make long strides toward healing only to be interrupted by life events; it felt like I was constantly breathing, expanding, collapsing, pausing, and returning but in a rough and tumble sort of way. I relearned a lot of what it meant to feel safe in my body after sexual and physical abuse. I had begun to reclaim who I was once I received the proper therapy and allowed safe connections in my life.

Befriending the traumatized parts of myself that would often scream at me to ruin my relationship, convincing me that I was chronically unsafe and thrived off self-rejection, or the ones who blamed self for everything that happened to me, started to retreat, and loosen their hold on me. All these experiences were hard lessons in life but drove me to heal, and eventually connect to an authentic version of myself. I spent too many years hyper-attuned to my environment and who was going to harm me that I lost time of awareness of who and what I was aligned with.

There was grief too—so much of it at times. Not just for the people I had lost throughout my life but for the time I lost. For the years I just spent surviving, watching the world and my experiences like they were happening through a fog. I grieved the relationships I had that I couldn't fully show up for, the connection I didn't feel throughout the years of severe symptoms. I learned to listen to my body again, to listen without running away, to believe that even the most broken parts of me had an important message.

Honestly, AA led me to feel that I was "fucked" forever and held to such limited restraints that I would always live from the stance that I was a drug addict and alcoholic. As

I grew emotionally, I realized that there was so much more to me than that and more to my story than a young woman who got clean and sober. While I am still sober and have no intention of returning to alcohol or drugs, my identity isn't rooted in what I once was.

I kept a lot of what happened to me during addiction private from my parents. I knew my dad's heart could not handle what he couldn't prevent or stop during my abusive relationship. He carried an unsurmountable amount of guilt from our childhood and years of turbulence when my parents were divorcing. He mostly verbalized this pain through writing and emails, a way to communicate for him without being overcome by intense emotions.

My mom, while aware of some, remained "unaware" for her own mental protection. Over time, I understood this. I began to recognize that she and I were not that different in our coping skills with extreme stress and trauma.

Over the years of my medical complications, my parents and stepparents all became one working unit. When Atticus was born and life seemed too delicate, something happened to all of us: everyone softened and focused on this little boy who needed us all. This newfound functioning family unit continued to grow through the birth of two more grandchildren, my brother's wedding, his various life events and struggles, my medical journey, happenings in all four of my parents' lives, shared space, and even a few golf games.

Watching my parents now, I see how much has changed. Despite the difficulties and dysfunction in childhood, they have become loving and attentive grandparents. They have been given a chance to do things differently with their grandchildren, and it has been healing to watch that unfold.

Kyle and I have worked hard to create a meaningful life for ourselves and our kids. We love to travel to connect as a family, whether it's a quick weekend trip or a long journey to a country across the world. As parents, we try to be intentional and mindful, using different parenting approaches than the ones we grew up with. We make mistakes but we continue to come back with newfound awareness and apologies if needed.

Our work has also become an important part of our story. Together, Kyle and I run a mental health facility that specializes in PTSD, complex trauma, and dissociative disorder. Every day we meet people who have been overlooked, misdiagnosed, or misunderstood. Helping them find the language for their pain discover a path toward healing has given our lives a deeper sense of purpose.

# acknowledgments

To the team at Authors Who Lead—you were willing to hear pieces of a puzzle and help me turn these pieces into something tangible and complete. Your team understood my goal, utilized my voice throughout the entire project without ever changing my true voice.

With gratitude, I want to acknowledge the cheerleaders in my life, professional and personal. The ones who took time to ask about my writing process, acknowledging the bravery that it takes to put your own life down on paper for everyone to read.

To my parents, stepparents, and brother. Although our journey to becoming a "stable enough" family unit has been full of challenges, time apart, and many tears—I am grateful for the feedback, listening ear, and "fill in" memory you have all provided in the development of my memoir. Thank you for allowing me to include you in my story.

To my best friends, the anchors in my life for as long as I can remember—there aren't enough words to express what our friendship means to me. We have grown up together- through heartache, tragedy, life changes, success, and growing into moms; we have done it all together and I would never change that for anything.

Throughout the events discussed in my story, you all have stayed by my side emotionally, despite being separated by countries; you always celebrated every milestone with me—you knew the importance of me healing because you experienced *my wounds* for years.

To the healing professionals who I have worked with intently; you truly saved my life. You provided me with healthy connection, you guided me to understand my dissociative symptoms, to befriend my nervous system, and taught me how to connect with my mind and body again. You held space for the intense pain, the tears, and my journey as I reconnected with myself.

meet chelsey

Chelsey Valeri is a mom, a wife, and a lifelong traveler who believes in living fully through every season of healing and change. She and her husband have spent fifteen years supporting each other through early addiction recovery and raising two spirited boys. At home, she is usually surrounded by her dogs, a warm cup of coffee, a puzzle, and a good book.

Chelsey is also a Licensed Clinical Social Worker with advanced training in trauma therapy. In her debut memoir, *Healed Enough: A Journey Through Complex Trauma and Dissociation*, she weaves her clinical understanding with her lived experience, offering a story told with clarity, candor, and deep compassion.

I would appreciate your feedback on what chapters helped you most and what you would like to see in future books.

If you enjoyed this book and found it helpful, please leave a review on Amazon.

Visit me at

CHELSEYVALERI.COM

where you can sign up for email updates.

thank you!